INDIANA UNIVERSITY BASKETBALL

For the Thrill of It!

MELANIE TOLLIVER

Front Cover Photos:
Mike Davis: Photo provided courtesy of AP/Wide World Photos.
Isiah Thomas and Bob Knight: Photo provided courtesy of The Associated Press.
Scott May and Quinn Buckner: Photo provided courtesy of Indiana University Archives.
Steve Alford and Daryl Thomas: Photo provided courtesy of Indiana University Archives.
Dane Fife: Photo provided courtesy of Doug Pensinger/Getty Images.

Back Cover Photo:
Photo provided courtesy of Paul Riley, IU Athletics Photography. Image Copyright Indiana University Athletics. Image may not be sold or redistributed without the express written consent of Indiana University Athletics.

Interior Photos:
Pages 2, 110, 118, 144, 145, 146, 147, 148, 149, and 150 (Kyle Hornsby): Photos provided courtesy of Paul Riley, IU Athletics Photography. Images Copyright Indiana University Athletics. Images may not be sold or redistributed without the express written consent of Indiana University Athletics.
Page 4: Photo provided courtesy of Marge Turley and Kelley Bailey.
Pages 5, 8, 9, 10, 12, 13, 15, 16, 18, 19, 20, 21, 22, 24, 25, 26, 28, 31, 32, 36, 38, 39, 40, 41, 42, 44, 46, 47, 48, 50, 51, 52, 54, 56, 57, 58, 59, 60, 62, 63, 64, 65, 66, 67, 69, 70, 74, 75, 76, 77, 80, 82, 83, 84, 86, 87, 88, 89, 90, 91, 92, 94, 95, 96, 98, 99, 100, 102, 103, 104, 106, 107, 108, 113, 114, 120, 122, 124, 125, 126, 128, 130, 131, 132, 133, 135, 136 (insets), and 140: Photos provided courtesy of Indiana University Archives.
Page 72: Photo provided courtesy of *The Bloomington Herald Times.*
Pages 112, 115, 136 (middle): Photos provided courtesy of Melanie Tolliver.
Pages 138, 150 (Antoine Davis): Photos provided courtesy of AP/Wide World Photos.
Page 142: Photo provided courtesy of Craig Jones/Getty Images.
Page 151: Photo provided courtesy of Doug Pensinger/Getty Images.

Interior Art:
Pages 6-7: "Tough Ticket," by Jon Onion.

Newspaper Articles:
Page 97: The Associated Press. 1987. "Film makers choose I.U. over Oscars." *Indianapolis News* (March 31): 12. Reprinted by permission of The Associated Press.
Page 30: Cone, Allen. 1975. "Rush hits McDonald's." *The Indiana Daily Student* (January 13). Reprinted, with permission, from *The Indiana Daily Student.*
Page 5: Keating, Thomas. 1976. "He's a R-r-real I.U. F-f-fan!" *The Indianapolis Star* (January 12). Reprinted, with permission, from *The Indianapolis Star.*

Director of production: Susan M. Moyer
Project manager: Tracy Gaudreau
Developmental editor: Mark E. Zulauf
Copy editor: Cindy McNew
Dust jacket design: Joseph Brumleve
Interior design: Jennifer Polson

ISBN: 1-58261-579-9
Printed in the United States of America

Sports Publishing L.L.C.
www.sportspublishingllc.com

With love and appreciation to my husband, Kevin Tolliver; my children, Chad, Josh, Jordan, and Ashley; my agent and friend, J. Andy Murphy; and the rest of my family and friends for their encouragement, love, and total support.

Table of Contents

Acknowledgments

The following individuals deserve a special note of thanks for their help in the realization of this book:

Bradley D. Cook, Reference Specialist and Photograph Curator, Indiana University Archives

Jeff Fanter, Indiana University Director of Media Relations

Beth Feickert, Indiana University Athletic Media Relations

Pete Rhoda, Indiana University Athletic Media Relations

B. J. McElroy, Indiana University Men's Basketball Office

Jennifer Brinnegar, Indiana University Athletics Compliance

Elizabeth Tompkins, Photo Solutions, Bloomington, IN

Mike Roberts, Indiana University Athletic Ticket Office

Dave Snodgress, Photographer, *Bloomington Herald Times*

Bob Zaltsberg, Editor, *Bloomington Herald Times*

The author would also like to thank the following Hoosiers for kindly sharing their time, insight, and memories:

Tom Abernethy	Kit Klingelhofer
Steve Alford	Todd Leary
Mike Davis	Scott May
Dane Fife	Sonnie Sicklesmith McCauley
Don Fischer	Keith Smart
Chuck Franz	Jim Thomas
Steve Green	Frank Wilson
Alan Henderson	

1
PASSION

The Essence of an IU Fan

THEY come in all shapes and sizes . . .
thirty pounds to three hundred . . .
ages three to eighty-three and older.
They are clerks, CEOs, farmers, teachers,
preachers, lawyers, rock stars and
grandmothers. Scattered across the
United States, this eclectic mass of
people share one common bond:
They love Indiana University basketball.

Through the years they have experienced the highest of highs as Hoosier teams have claimed college basketball's most valued prize. Disappointments and trying times have sometimes accompanied the ride. Yet it is the pursuit of basketball excellence and the thrill of the journey that keep Indiana fans passionate about their team.

Every November brings renewed interest and anticipation of upcoming moments of exhilaration. The heat and excitement of game nights in front of the TV shorten the cold, long winter months. And in March, the calendars of IU fans are cleared in hope that breathtaking memories of success will be part of approaching days.

BELOW
An hour and a half drive and winter weather don't keep Marge Turley and Kelly Bailey from cheering on the Hoosiers.

A Fan's Perspective

Friends know to NEVER call our home during an IU game.
—Melanie Tolliver

He's a R-r-real IU F-f-fan!
Thomas R. Keating

WHEN YOU'RE a basketball fan in Indiana nothing gets in your way.

A week ago Saturday night, Walter Dake, a 53-year-old Boggstown area resident, got all his chores out of the way, turned out all the lights and settled into the back bedroom of his home.

He wanted no distractions as he and his wife watched Indiana University start its Big Ten basketball title defense against Ohio State on television.

With the game midway through the first half, Dake heard a noise outside but ignored it, concentrating instead on a way for Kent Benson to get loose inside and break the unusual zone the Buckeyes were employing.

A few minutes later, as Dake was coaxing Bobby Knight to fire up his squad, there was a loud knock at the door.

Mumbling to himself about interruptions at the wrong time, Dake started to the door but happened to glance out a side window and notice a man fooling around with two 300-gallon fuel storage tanks near the driveway.

Instead of answering the knock, Dake kept quiet, figuring correctly that his tanks were being burglarized and the man at the door, seeing no lights on inside, was checking to make sure no one was home.

Catching a glimpse of Quinn Buckner scoring on a layup, Dake grabbed his .22 caliber rifle, cranked in a few rounds and raced out on the porch in his underwear.

To get everyone's attention, Dake fired one round in the air and told the three men ready to steal his fuel to raise their hands and freeze.

They did—and so eventually did Dake, because he forgot to put on even a pair of socks in the 15-degree weather.

While Dake held his rifle on the intruders, he told his wife to call the Shelby County Sheriff and turn up the I.U. game in that order. Well, we like to think it was in that order.

And then, for the next 25 minutes, while the sheriff's deputies and state police were en route, Dake stood barefoot in his skivvies on a corner of his porch and trained the rifle on the would-be thieves.

He told police later that he had stood on the porch, far across the yard from the three men he had caught, so they could not see him.

But that way he also could still hear the IU game while the law was on the way.

"The three men were arrested, I eventually thawed out, and most important, Indiana beat Ohio State," Dake said. "Neither my wife nor I ever miss an IU game on television and I'll tell you, we didn't intend to."

9

A handful of players made the move from the New Fieldhouse to Assembly Hall. Guard Frank Wilson, who played in both facilities, has positive memories about the Fieldhouse. He fondly recalls kicking and scraping sawdust off his shoes after running from the locker room to the playing floor and then jumping up about three feet to get onto the floor. Noise generated by the student body stomping on the wooden bleachers helped create a homecourt advantage. That homecourt advantage was eventually transferred to Assembly Hall.

The community and the players anticipated moving to the new facility with delight. The new floor and phenomenal locker rooms, along with the "glitz and the glamour" of Assembly Hall, are cited by Wilson as high points of the new address.

From a spectator's point of view, Assembly Hall leaves much to be desired. With steep stairs and an obscured view of the scoreboard from some seats, fans feel far from the court, especially if they sit in the balcony. As Kit Klingelhofer, associate athletic director and former media relations director, says: "It's not a great spectator facility by any stretch of the imagination. But it's always had kind of an aura. You know, a lot of teams come in here intimidated. Now, obviously, the strength of our teams down through the years, without question, contributed to that … especially, probably, the first 20 years. I think that invincibility wore off maybe over the last 10 years. But I think for 20 years there was such an aura of teams coming in—especially nonconference teams, kids that have never played here before—they'd come in and see all the banners hanging up, because, from the floor looking up, it's very impressive …You walk in here as a visiting team and have never seen this place and then run out in front of 17,000 fans and see the banners and see everybody in red, and the excitement—I think there is really an aura surrounding this building that, I think, still exists."

There must be something to that "aura." Since Assembly Hall opened in December of 1971, the homecourt record stands at 372 wins against 52 losses, an 88 percent winning record.

A Player Remembers

"I've, to this day, only been in the balcony one time in my life. I went up and visited there early. I think it was probably my first year. And I never went back. I mean, it was so far up. I went, 'Whoa. Wait a minute.' So I always had just a real fond feeling for those people that would pack Assembly Hall. We'd set these records of attendance. I'd look up. We're not setting those records without people sitting in those seats up there. And it was really special."

—Steve Green
Forward, 1971 – 1975
All-American, 1974, 1975

**OPPOSITE
LEFT**
Steel beams and millions of pounds
of concrete created a rock-solid
building—in structure and tradition.

ABOVE
While minor adjustments are
made to the scoreboard in the
Hoosiers' new home, director
Ray Kramer leads the Pep Band.

3
1971 – 1972
Dawn of a New Era

AN epoch began on December 1, 1971. It was the day of a new home, a new coach, a new era. The tip of the first ball as the Hoosiers took on Ball State marked the awakening of an age of distinction and glory in IU's already storied basketball tradition.

The opening game was the unveiling of a beautiful new facility for the home team as well as for the visitors. Final finishing phases of construction kept IU practices in the Fieldhouse until a few weeks before the first game.

A young Robert Montgomery Knight became the 24th coach of Indiana University basketball and began what was to become a legendary reign at the helm. He had spent six years leading Army to a winning record. At age 31, he inherited a roster of ten and the tension of the 1970 season.

Bob Knight brought with him a new style of play. Defense was the name of the game. Always known as the "Hurrying Hoosiers," the new emphasis on defense brought a dramatic change to the IU game. Because Indiana had averaged 90.8 points a game in the '70-71 season, Hoosier fans had trouble adjusting to the slower, defensive mode when the average points per game dropped to 73.6. "You'd hear rumblings in the stands because Coach Knight ran kind of a patient offense, especially that first year. People had been used to that run-and-gun basketball, and ... there were people in the stands yelling 'shoot' a lot of times or you'd hear murmured even some boos when we'd slow down play," recalls associate athletic director Kit Klingelhofer. "You know, winning cures all, and once people found out the new system started working pretty well, then people kind of converted over—but they just weren't used to seeing slow-down basketball."

The season of *firsts* brought credibility and glimpses of future success.

ABOVE
A young Bob Knight takes his position for the first of twenty-nine seasons.

It seems fitting that the first game in Assembly Hall, an 84-77 victory over Ball State, was highlighted by junior Steve Downing's performance of 26 rebounds, an Assembly Hall record that still stands today. After opening the season with three wins, the Hoosiers and new Coach Knight battled a seventh-ranked Kentucky team to a nail-biting double overtime 90-89 victory in Freedom Hall.

A game still remembered by players and fans alike is the dedication game of Assembly Hall on December 18, 1971. Featuring two first-year coaches, Bob Knight and Digger Phelps of Notre Dame, the end result was the largest margin of victory by an Indiana team in the history of IU basketball. The sixty-five-point 94-29 win caused confusion for newspapers and broadcasters who thought surely the correct score was 94-92. Hoosier John Ritter outscored the entire Notre Dame team 31-29.

The season closed with promise, an overall record of 17-8, and a tie for third place in the Big Ten. Although they went one game and out, the opportunity to play in New York at the National Invitational Tournament was welcomed. It had been five years since an Indiana basketball team had qualified for postseason play.

LEFT
Steve Downing's record of 26 rebounds was established in the first game at Assembly Hall.

A Player Remembers

"I always say we became the *Harassing Hoosiers.* If we scored 60 points a game it would be fine for Bobby Knight. He didn't care. Defense was emphasized. The way I remember it, we didn't even have an offensive set play until two weeks before the season began. We spent the first official practices, the first four weeks, was all on defense and his rules. And his rules of defense are very complicated.

So here we all are, a bunch of guys who didn't even know how to spell defense, and now we're expected to play defense at a level we didn't think existed. So once we caught on, it really did disrupt a lot of teams."

—Frank Wilson,
when asked about the change from
Hurrying Hoosiers to a defensive focused team
Guard, 1970 – 1973
Academic All-Big Ten, 1972

RIGHT
The first official point
scored in Assembly Hall
was a free throw by
guard Frank Wilson.

A Fan's Perspective

"The first year of Assembly Hall, students were given a coupon book when they purchased season tickets. The week before each game you would exchange a coupon for a ticket at the Auditorium or at Assembly Hall. If you were in the student booster club, your seat was in the bleachers on the north end of the floor. There were no bleacher seats on the sides of the court the first few years."

Team Roster 1971-1972
(Overall 17-8, Big Ten 9-5,
Tied for Third in Conference)

#	Player	Pos.	Year
20	Frank Wilson	G	J
22	Bootsie White	G	J
23	Steve Heiniger	G	So
24	Dave Shepherd	G	So
32	Steve Downing	C	J
33	Jerry Memering	C	J
42	John Ritter	G/F	J
43	Rick Ford	F	S
44	Joby Wright	F	S
54	Kim Pemberton	G	J

ABOVE
The 1972 – 1973
Indiana Hoosiers.

4
1972 – 1973

Freshmen, Fate and the Final Four

WHEN the NCAA rule change allowed freshmen to play on the varsity level in the fall of 1972, the foundation was laid for the most successful class of players in IU basketball history. Highly touted Quinn Buckner along with Jim Crews and Tom Abernethy were the core of the seven freshman recruits affected. They joined six sophomores, featuring Steve Green and John Laskowski, who had experienced success on the freshman team. With the varsity players of '72, the team roster expanded to twenty.

With John Ritter and Steve Downing leading the way, the Hoosiers rolled into the Big Ten looking strong. Only four games remained in the season and their record showed only three conference losses. IU stood in third place behind defending champion and heavily favored Minnesota.

The season culminated with a bizarre chain of events. A surprise upset of Minnesota by Iowa set up the final game in Assembly Hall against Purdue. A victory would ensure a tie with Minnesota for the Big Ten title. The victory happened. What was not anticipated was another shocking upset of Minnesota by lowly 1-12 Northwestern. Bob Knight and team had their first Big Ten title in the Assembly Hall era and a spot in the NCAA Tournament.

The NCAA Regionals were played in Nashville, where the Hoosiers defeated Marquette and Kentucky and advanced to the Final Four. In those days, making it to the Final Four was one of the few ways to make it onto national television. There was no ESPN or Big Ten Game of the Week. Indiana had made it to the big time in terms of national exposure.

Team Roster 1972-1973*
(Overall 22-6, Big Ten 11-3,
First in Conference)

#	Player	Pos.	Year
20	Frank Wilson	G	S
21	Quinn Buckner	G	F
22	Trent Smock	F	F
23	Steve Heiniger	G	J
24	Steve Ahlfeld	G	So
25	Doug Allen	F	So
30	John Kamstra	G	So
31	John Laskowski	G	So
32	Steve Downing	C	S
33	Jerry Memering	F/C	S
34	Steve Green	F	So
41	Craig Morris	G	F
42	John Ritter	F	S
43	Don Noort	F/C	F
45	Jim Crews	G	F
54	Tom Abernethy	F	F

*Bootsie White, John Hunter, Mike Miller and Kim Pemberton were listed on the original roster but did not complete the season

BELOW
Downing was named All-American in 1973.

RIGHT
In his second year as head coach, Bob Knight addresses a gathering of grateful fans following the '73 Final Four appearance.

The meeting of No. 1-ranked UCLA and IU was a battle which pitted big man Steve Downing against college basketball's premier player, Bill Walton. The Hoosiers battled from a 22-point deficit to close the gap to three. Then, still-remembered fouls called on Downing rather than Walton, and a final score of 59-70, ended the dream of another Hoosier national title.

The successful season of 1973, the Big Ten title and the unexpected trip to the Final Four set the stage for the upcoming acts of the underclassmen.

A Player Remembers

"It was the only time, after that first game in Assembly Hall, in my collegiate career that I had that same feeling of just being out of body. It was just too much. You know, it was … oh my gosh, this is the Final Four. I'm finally here. I've dreamed about it. Just couldn't really feel my fingers or toes or anything like that."

—Steve Green on the 1973 trip to the Final Four
Forward, 1971 – 1975

LEFT
John Ritter and Steve Downing proudly display the third-place NCAA trophy.

RIGHT
Coach Knight confers with his first recruit, Steve Green.

5
1973 – 1974

CCA Champs:
A Dubious Distinction

COMING off the flurry of success at the end of the '72-73 season, the Hoosiers had national attention and a higher level of expectation as they entered the new season. Freshman Mr. Basketball Kent Benson joined sophomores Bobby Wilkerson and Scott May as newcomers to the roster.

Preconference play got off to a decent start, losing only to sixth ranked Notre Dame with John Schumate and Adrian Dantley and to Oregon State in the Far West Classic. In January, Big Ten play opened with a loss to conference challenger Michigan. For the next two months, excitement built as the Hoosiers went on to record twelve consecutive victories.

LEFT
Over the years,
fans witnessed this
scene a few times.

The last home game of the year, against Purdue, proved the thriller of the season. Down by ten midway through the second half, IU gained the lead with eight seconds left and claimed victory. The win gave them the Big Ten title, shared with cochampion Michigan. Only one Big Ten team could advance to the NCAA Tournament, and a 67-75 loss in the playoff game held in Champaign gave that spot to Michigan.

Normally IU would have been given the opportunity to play in the respected National Invitational Tournament.

In 1974, however, the Collegiate Commissioners' Association Tournament was newly established. The idea was to create an esteemed tournament for teams who finished second in their conference.

On the flight back from Champaign to Bloomington, Coach Knight called junior Steve Green to the front of the plane. Explaining that it wasn't his desire to go to this new "losers' tournament," he asked Steve to talk with the team and get their input. Steve recalls holding a players' meeting the next day at McNutt Quad, where an upside-down opened umbrella was used to collect the votes. The team agreed not to go.

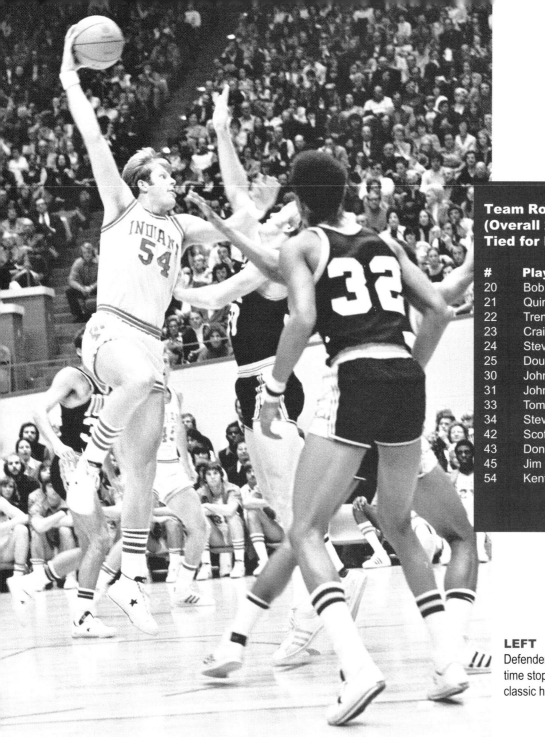

Team Roster 1973-1974
(Overall 23-5, Big Ten 12-2,
Tied for First in Conference)

#	Player	Pos.	Year
20	Bob Wilkerson	G	So
21	Quinn Buckner	G	So
22	Trent Smock	F	So
23	Craig Morris	G	So
24	Steve Ahlfeld	G	J
25	Doug Allen	F	J
30	John Kamstra	G	J
31	John Laskowski	G/F	J
33	Tom Abernethy	F	So
34	Steve Green	F	J
42	Scott May	F	So
43	Don Noort	C	So
45	Jim Crews	G	So
54	Kent Benson	C	F

LEFT
Defenders had a hard
time stopping Benson's
classic hook shot.

Trotting over to Assembly Hall, Steve reported the result of the vote to the coach, who then suggested that playing in the CCA tournament would give Benson the experience of three more games and would allow the university to fulfill its obligation to appear in the fledgling tournament. "Share these thoughts with the team and have another vote," were the coach's instructions. The team again voted to skip the tournament. This time, Knight's response was, "I appreciate that, but we're going."

The agony and the ecstasy of the season occurred in one game at Purdue in a battle to clench the Big Ten championship. In the first half, All-American Scott May broke his left arm. Senior John Laskowski took May's spot on the floor, and the rest of the game was a classic. In a nail-biter to the end, Steve Green scored 29 points. Added to the strong numbers posted by the rest of the squad, the Boilers were defeated 83-82, and for the third straight year Indiana became conference champions. The Hoosiers had claimed the crown and achieved their first victory ever in Mackey Arena yet left feeling down because they had lost the play of their friend and teammate.

With four games remaining in the regular season, adjustments were made. Laskowski continued to play well, and the team advanced to the regional finals of the NCAA Tournament with convincing victories.

When IU met Kentucky in on March 22, 1975, Scott May was to start for the first time since his injury. Hopes and confidence of the Hoosier faithful were crushed when the UK team remembered the trouncing they took earlier in the season at Assembly Hall and defeated IU 92-90.

Shocked and stunned, Hoosier fans drove home from Dayton in silence. In retrospect, the season still shines as one of the most dominant years of any IU team. Ranked No. 1 for eleven weeks and finishing with a 31-1 record, the 1974-1975 team is deserving of a place of high esteem in the annals of Hoosier basketball.

LEFT
Fans eagerly awaited May's return.

Team Roster 1974-1975 (Overall 31-1, Big Ten 18-0, First in Conference)

#	Player	Pos.	Year
20	Bob Wilkerson	G/F	J
21	Quinn Buckner	G	J
22	Wayne Radford	G/F	F
24	Steve Ahlfeld	G	S
25	Doug Allen	F	S
30	John Kamstra	G	S
31	John Laskowski	G/F	S
32	Mark Haymore	F/C	F
33	Tom Abernethy	F	J
34	Steve Green	F	S
40	Jim Wisman	G	F
42	Scott May	F	J
43	Don Noort	C	J
45	Jim Crews	G	J
54	Kent Benson	C	So

A Player Remembers

"When he [John Ritter] was introduced for the starting lineup, he would pat Coach Knight a certain way on his left shoulder. He'd be passing and patting. And Ritter took me aside and told me, 'Now look, when I'm gone next year, you've got to do this.' It was something he handed down. I said, 'What are you talking about?' He said, 'Well, yeah, you've got to do that. That's good luck.'

And so we did. That was at any place. But I always remember the big games at Assembly Hall. The big afternoon games. We're playing Michigan. We're playing Purdue. It was such a thrill, and it always gave me that feeling of calm because even though it was a big game, we'd do this. It was the last calm thing, if you will, to remind you that everything's going to be fine."

—Steve Green
Forward, 1971 – 1975
All American, 1974, 1975

A Fan's Perspective

"My husband called me at work to tell me that the polls had just come out and we were ranked No. 1. We couldn't believe it. In our lifetime, we thought only UCLA could be No.1. Now it was us! What a thrill. In a few days, fans everywhere were wearing buttons saying 'Indiana #1.'"

IU IQ

Assembly Hall opened in:
a. 1970
b. 1971
c. 1972
d. 1973

The name of the basketball court in Assembly Hall is:
a. Old Fieldhouse Floor
b. Robert Knight Court
c. McCracken Memorial Court
d. Hoosier Memorial Court

What '71-72 player is second in IU basketball history for career free throw percentage?
a. Steve Downing
b. Dave Shepherd
c. John Ritter
d. Joby Wright

Who was the assist leader on the '71-72 team?
a. Bootsie White
b. John Ritter
c. Frank Wilson
d. Rick Ford

Which member of the '71-72 team later became an assistant coach?

A member of the '72-73 team was named Big Ten MVP, the first since 1958. Who was it?
a. John Ritter
b. Frank Wilson
c. Steve Downing
d. Quinn Buckner

The current venue of IU basketball was named Assembly Hall because:

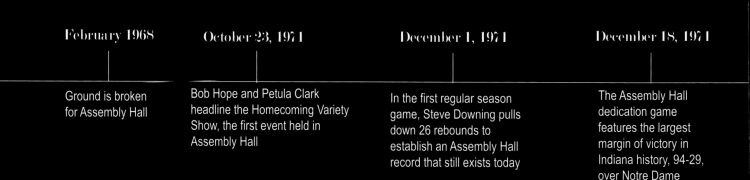

February 1968	October 23, 1971	December 1, 1971	December 18, 1971
Ground is broken for Assembly Hall	Bob Hope and Petula Clark headline the Homecoming Variety Show, the first event held in Assembly Hall	In the first regular season game, Steve Downing pulls down 26 rebounds to establish an Assembly Hall record that still exists today	The Assembly Hall dedication game features the largest margin of victory in Indiana history, 94-29, over Notre Dame

IU IQ

The first year Bob Knight was named Big Ten Coach of the Year was:
  a. 1971
  b. 1972
  c. 1973
  d. 1974

The player with the most assists on the '73-74 team was:
  a. Jim Crews
  b. Quinn Buckner
  c. John Laskowski
  d. Bob Wilkerson

Who were the team captains on the '73-74 team?

The '74-75 team leads all other Hoosier teams in which category?
  a. rebounds
  b. assists
  c. blocks
  d. steals

Which team leads all other Hoosier teams in field goal attempts and field goals made?
  a. '74-75
  b. '75-76
  c. '80-81
  d. '92-93

The leading scorer on the '73-74 team was:
  a. Steve Green
  b. Scott May
  c. John Laskowski
  d. Kent Benson

Answers: b. 1971; c. McCracken Memorial Court (Named after Branch McCracken); C. John Ritter (.908); a. Bootsie White (104 assists); Joby Wright; c. Steve Downing; IU's first home was in "Assembly Hall", built in the 1840s; c. 1973; b.Quinn Buckner; Steve Green and Quinn Buckner; a. rebounds (1433 total/ 70 more than any other team); a. '74-75; a. Steve Green

March 10, 1973	March 9, 1974	March 18, 1974	March 8, 1975
First Senior Day is held on the Assembly Hall court following defeat of Purdue and winning of Big Ten title	IU claims Big Ten title in Assembly Hall with thrilling victory over Purdue	The Hoosiers claim CCA Tournament in St. Louis with victory over USC	The largest crowd (17,912) in IU's history witnesses a home victory over Michigan State; Indiana claims its third consecutive Big Ten Championship

After a victory over Florida State, Notre Dame came calling at Assembly Hall and provided a tough challenge, but fell 63-60. The Kentucky game that followed was played at Freedom Hall in Louisville and, to this day, is one that stands out in Indiana basketball history. Down by two, the Hoosiers inbounded with 29 seconds remaining. Passes ensued, and then Kentucky's Rick Robey interfered with Tom Abernethy's shot and the ball was deflected. Kent Benson stuck out his hand for a tip-in, and with nine seconds left, the ball went through the hoop and tied the game. Once into overtime, IU gained the victory, 77-68. The thrilling end of regulation play kept the dream of a perfect record alive.

Following with five more wins, the opening game of the Big Ten season provided the next heart stopper for Indiana. At Ohio State in Columbus, the Buckeyes and crowd were fired up and challenged IU down to the last second of the game. Final score: 66-64 Indiana. Another near loss averted.

The third in a trilogy of close calls took place on February 7, 1976. The Michigan Wolverines came into Assembly Hall and smelled blood after a poor offensive start by IU. At halftime the home team trailed 39-29. Halfway into the second half, Michigan maintained an eight-point lead. Sophomore Wayne Radford provided a spark, but with ten seconds remaining, the Hoosiers trailed by two. Buckner shot and missed. Jim Crews rebounded, shot and missed. Once again, Kent Benson's rebound tip-in tied the game with 0 seconds showing on the clock. The crowd roared and the dream lived on.

After claiming the Big Ten title, the team approached the NCAA Tournament with cautious optimism. The ultimate goal was yet to be achieved. The first game of the tournament was played in South Bend where a twenty-point victory over St. John's was witnessed by an arena full of red-clad IU supporters. The remainder of the path to the prize was blocked by sixth- ranked Alabama, second-ranked Marquette, fifth-ranked UCLA, and ninth-ranked Michigan.

Alabama provided the closest of the challenges. IU was off to a quick start and maintained control most of the game. Alabama came back to grab a one-point lead with 3:58 left before Tom Abernethy and Scott May stepped up to ensure the win for IU, 74-69. Next, Indiana conquered coach Al McGuire and the Marquette crew, 65-56, after playing a tough first half. The Hoosiers advanced to the Final Four in Philadelphia and the hopes continued.

RIGHT
Tom Abernethy's outstanding play was rewarded by a place on the All-Final Four Team.

**Team Roster 1975-1976
(Overall 32-0, Big Ten 18-0,
First in Conference)**

#	Player	Pos.	Year
20	Bob Wilkerson	G	S
21	Quinn Buckner	G	S
22	Wayne Radford	G/F	So
23	Jim Wisman	G	So
25	Bob Bender	G	F
31	Scott Eells	F	F
32	Mark Haymore	F/C	So
33	Tom Abernethy	F	S
34	Rich Valavicius	F	F
42	Scott May	F	S
43	Jim Roberson	F/C	F
45	Jim Crews	G	S
54	Kent Benson	C	J

After the loss to IU in November, vengeance-minded Bruin players expressed their desire to play the Hoosiers at season's end. The first game of the Final Four provided that opportunity. The attempt failed, with Tom Abernethy playing excellent defense when called to guard All-American Richard Washington.

The City of Brotherly Love provided the backdrop for the season's third meeting of conference rivals Michigan and Indiana. In a game where the lead frequently changed hands, IU saw senior Bobby Wilkerson knocked unconscious only two minutes and 43 seconds into the game. He departed on a stretcher, and faithful followers wondered if an injury would again affect the outcome of another season. Jim Crews replaced Wilkerson, and the Hoosiers carried on. Down at the half, the game remained close until IU took over midway through the second half with contributions from all on the floor. The largest contributors were Benson, who had nine rebounds and 25 points, and Scott May, who finished with eight rebounds and 26 points.

Once the outcome, and victory, was apparent, Bob Knight brought the dancing starters out one at a time. Together, coach and player embraced, sharing the emotion of past years. Those moments will be remembered and treasured by those fortunate folk who witnessed the special sight. Years of hard work and determination and perseverance netted the prize—the national championship and an undefeated season.

The seniors on the '76 team accomplished the following: four Big Ten Titles, a CCA Tournament Championship, two Final Four appearances, a NCAA Championship, and a four-year record of 108-12.

They are the last Division One NCAA team to have an undefeated season. They will not be forgotten!

A Player Remembers

"I don't know if we ever would admit that there was pressure, but there had to have been pressure on us. Again, there was a huge target on us. If someone could beat us, it would be great. So maybe we didn't play at certain times as well as maybe we could, but I think we brought the best out of our opponents. At least they wanted to give us a good shot.

Individually, there were probably games when every one of us did not play well. But that's what made us a good team. One or two guys not playing well didn't sink the ship. We had enough guys on that team that could step up. So there was probably pressure; I don't think we dwelled on it. Coach Knight certainly didn't allow that to be a thing we focused on."

—Tom Abernethy
Forward, 1972 – 1976
Final Four All-Tournament Team, 1976

A Fan's Perspective

"The atmosphere the entire '75-76 season was awesome. While the teams warmed up during pregame, the Pep Band would play 'Mighty Quinn,' and it seemed like every person in Assembly Hall was standing, clapping and swaying to the song.

That was followed by the tipoff, where Bobby Wilkerson, our guard, would outjump the center of almost every opposing team. How intimidating! It was a truly incredible year."

A Broadcaster Remembers

"Probably the most memorable, as far as any particular game is concerned, was the championship game in 1976 when IU won it all. That team, to me, had overcome so many obstacles and so many difficulties. Yet through it all, they never lost.

They were able to survive two overtimes that year against Kentucky and against Michigan by miracle tip-ins, both by Kent Benson—and then, of course, win in overtime.

This group of kids rarely showed much emotion. But the last minute of that game, when Coach Knight started to take the players out one at a time, putting somebody else in … that became such an emotional time. …When I go back and listen to that game, I still get tears welling up. You know, it's just special.

To watch that team celebrate like they did, to me, that's one of the most memorable moments I'll ever have. It's always special when it's the first time, and that was my first NCAA Championship broadcast."

—Don Fischer
Indiana Sportscaster of the Year on 22 occasions

**Team Roster 1976–1977
(Overall 16-11, Big Ten 11-7,
Fifth in Conference)**

#	Player	Pos.	Year
20	Bill Cunningham	G	F
22	Wayne Radford	G/F	J
23	Jim Wisman	G	J
31	Scott Eells	F	So
33	Trent Smock	G/F	S
34	Rich Valavicius	F	So
40	Glen Grunwald	F	F
41	Butch Carter	G/F	F
42	Mike Woodson	G/F	F
43	Jim Roberson	F/C	So
44	Derek Holcomb	F/C	F
45	Mike Miday	F	F
54	Kent Benson	C	S

A bright point of the season was the debut of freshman Mike Woodson, from Broad Ripple High School in Indianapolis. Woodson showed great promise and completed the year as the leading team scorer.

Benson, fondly referred to as Big Red by fans, required back surgery and was forced to miss the last four games of the season. He closed his Hoosier career a three time All-American, a member of the All-Big Ten Team, an Academic All-American and Big Ten Most Valuable Player.

In the fall of '77, a fresh group of freshmen joined the Hoosier corps, bringing new life and hope. Off to a 2-1 start, they faced a solid No. 2-ranked Notre Dame team in Assembly Hall and surprisingly upset the Irish on a Wayne Radford free throw with four seconds showing on the clock.

Conference play began with three losses, but IU bounced back and closed the season strongly, with eight consecutive wins. As a result of their second-place Big Ten finish, they netted an invitation to the NCAA Tournament where they won the first game against Furman by one and lost the next game to Villanova by one.

RIGHT
Jim Wisman was a team captain his senior year.

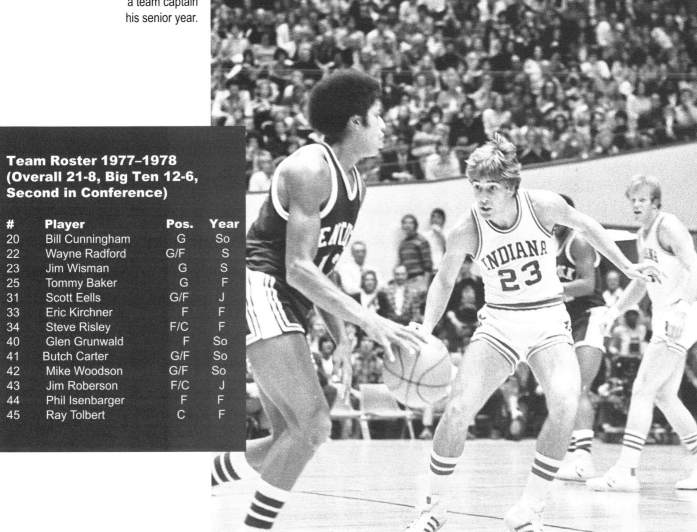

Team Roster 1977–1978
(Overall 21-8, Big Ten 12-6,
Second in Conference)

#	Player	Pos.	Year
20	Bill Cunningham	G	So
22	Wayne Radford	G/F	S
23	Jim Wisman	G	S
25	Tommy Baker	G	F
31	Scott Eells	G/F	J
33	Eric Kirchner	F	F
34	Steve Risley	F/C	F
40	Glen Grunwald	F	So
41	Butch Carter	G/F	So
42	Mike Woodson	G/F	So
43	Jim Roberson	F/C	J
44	Phil Isenbarger	F	F
45	Ray Tolbert	C	F

9
1978 – 1979

NIT Champs

THE Seawolf Classic in Anchorage was the backdrop for the disastrous start of a new season. Losing the first two games of the tournament, the Hoosiers bounced back to win the third and returned to Bloomington. The return brought the unpleasant dismissal of three players for marijuana use and probation for the remaining players. Where would the season go from there?

Things took a more positive turn when sixth-ranked Kentucky visited Assembly Hall. Expecting to roll over a .500 Indiana team, the Wildcats were surprised by an overtime 68-67 loss. Mike Woodson scored 27 points in the Indiana victory.

LEFT
Tolbert and Carter have a special addition for the trophy case in Assembly Hall.

Six games into Big Ten play, IU's conference record was 1-5, and they later found themselves in seventh place. The remainder of the season brought improved play and was highlighted by the final game at Illinois when Woodson singed the nets with 48 points. His performance in Champaign in 1979 still holds a place in the record book for the most points scored by any Bob Knight player. It also caused the NIT to take a second look at a team with an 18-12 record and issue the Hoosiers an invitation to the tournament.

After winning the first two games of the National Invitation Tournament, Indiana players and coaches were ready to head to the Big Apple. In New York, two familiar opponents awaited them, Big Ten schools Ohio State and, eventually, Purdue. Handling OSU 64-55, the Hoosiers turned their attention to archrival Purdue.

ABOVE
The background of the Big Apple silhouettes
freshman Randy Wittman as he enters
Madison Square Garden for the big game.

The two previous contests of the season between IU and PU were split. The match for the NIT crown proved worthy of the rivalry. With 21 seconds left, Purdue had the ball and the lead, 52-51. Butch Carter fouled Purdue All-American Joe Barry Carroll. Carroll missed the free throw and Ray Tolbert grabbed the rebound. A play designed for Mike Woodson didn't pan out, forcing Butch Carter to put up an 18-foot shot with four seconds left. It went in, and IU won the NIT Championship.

Also to be remembered in the final game are the outstanding defensive job freshman Landon Turner did on Carroll and the chess game played by head coaches Bob Knight and Lee Rose. In the last 30 seconds of the game, six time-outs were called.

LEFT
Indianapolis freshman Landon Turner, from Tech High School, showed promise and potential.

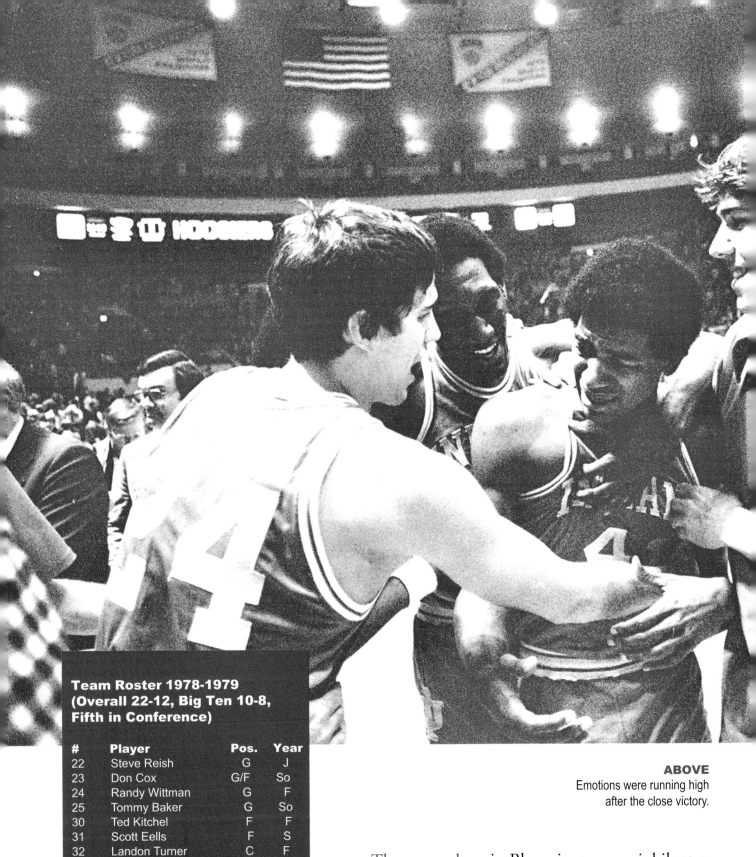

**Team Roster 1978-1979
(Overall 22-12, Big Ten 10-8,
Fifth in Conference)**

#	Player	Pos.	Year
22	Steve Reish	G	J
23	Don Cox	G/F	So
24	Randy Wittman	G	F
25	Tommy Baker	G	So
30	Ted Kitchel	F	F
31	Scott Eells	F	S
32	Landon Turner	C	F
33	Eric Kirchner	F	So
40	Glen Grunwald	F	J
41	Butch Carter	G	J
42	Mike Woodson	F	J
43	Jim Roberson	C	S
44	Phil Isenbarger	F	So
45	Ray Tolbert	C	So

ABOVE
Emotions were running high
after the close victory.

The atmosphere in Bloomington was jubilant as
students streamed to Showalter Fountain to celebrate.

A Fan's Perspective

"In 1979, long before IU dorm rooms had been rewired to accommodate computers, fax machines, microwaves, DVD players and televisions, students actually ventured into the dorm lounges to watch the one shared television—no cable and chained to the wall. I lived in McNutt, and we shared the corner lounge and TV with the adjacent guys' floor.

Nights of away IU basketball games found the lounge full, as most of us couldn't wait to cheer on the Hoosiers. It was very exciting that the team fought its way back and made it to the NIT finals.

The lounge was hot and crowded. What stands out is that Butch Carter made the shot that won the game. The room was deafeningly loud with cheers, screams and mass hysteria. I followed my friends down the stairs and down the street. I really didn't know where we were going, but I knew that I didn't want to miss it. The group on the street kept growing and growing until it was a mob. We arrived at Showalter Fountain in front of the auditorium. People were dancing with the fountain's sculptured dolphins, scaling the naked lady's breasts, climbing trees and just generally expressing joy! It was a late night, but a great one."

—Michele Calderon
Student, 1978 – 1982

10
1979 – 1980

The Big Ten Title and What Could Have Been

EYES were focused on Indiana as the '79-80 season began. Preseason polls ranked the team No. 1 in the nation. A successful 4-0 start had the Hoosier hopeful dreaming about possible titles and championships.

The trip to Kentucky brought an obstacle in the path to those dreams. Sophomore Randy Wittman suffered a season-ending foot stress fracture. IU lost that game 69-58. A week later, leading scorer Mike Woodson was lost to back surgery.

With the roster reduced by two, the Hoosiers battled on in the Big Ten, establishing a 7-5 conference record. Amazingly, a gutsy Woodson returned to the court seven weeks after surgery. It was one of those perfect moments sports fans dream of, as senior Woodson drilled his first three shots and tallied 20 points that night in his comeback appearance. Indiana defeated the Hawkeyes in Iowa City, 66-55. For the rest of the season, the Hoosiers never looked back, notching six consecutive wins.

The season finale is thought by some to be the best game played in Assembly Hall to date. Ohio State came in tied with IU for the conference title. On national television, fans witnessed a well played tough battle when Butch Carter calmly hit two free throws to force the game into overtime. Eventually the victory and Big Ten title were claimed by the Hoosiers, making Senior Day a real celebration.

Team Roster 1979-1980
(Overall 21-8, Big Ten 13-5,
First in Conference)

#	Player	Pos.	Year
11	Isiah Thomas	G	F
20	Jim Thomas	G	F
23	Chuck Franz	G	F
24	Randy Wittman	G	So
30	Ted Kitchel	F	So
31	Tony Brown	G	F
32	Landon Turner	F/C	So
34	Steve Risley	F	J
40	Glen Grunwald	F	S
41	Butch Carter	G	S
42	Mike Woodson	F	S
44	Phil Isenbarger	F	J
45	Ray Tolbert	C	J
54	Steve Bouchie	F	F

RIGHT
Woodson scored 21 points against OSU and played every minute of the overtime game.

The trip to the NCAA was short-lived, with a first-game win and then a loss to Purdue.

LEFT
Two clutch free throws by Carter forced the Ohio State game into overtime and eventually gave IU the Big Ten Championship.

RIGHT
Coach to future coach, the game plan is discussed.

An Associate Athletic Director Remembers

"I t'd obviously be tough to recreate the best game I've ever seen in here. But I think one—and I tell people this all the time—for what the game meant and the quality of opponents on the floor, I think the best game I've ever seen in here was—and again there's been a hundred and it's hard to pick out one—[when] we beat Ohio State in 1980 in the final game of the regular season.

We came in tied, played for the Big Ten Championship, and won in overtime. And I think on the floor, combined for Indiana and Ohio State, were seven players who went on to play in the NBA. I mean ... Isiah was on that team, [and] Ray Tolbert, Randy Wittman . . . They had Calvin Ramsey and Clark Kellogg and Herb Williams— I mean it was just an unbelievable array of talent on the floor. It was an unbelievable game we won in overtime. That would be one game that sticks out."

—Kit Klingelhofer
Indiana University Associate Athletic Director

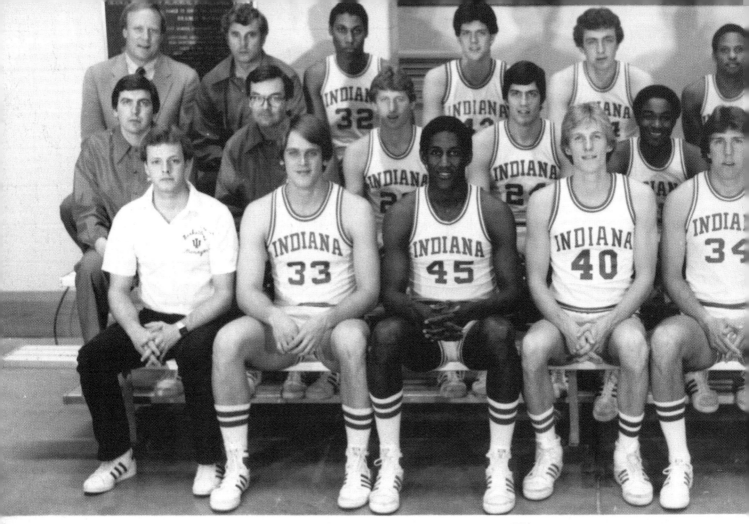

Hoosiers of '81

National Collegiate Champion

Indiana Classic Champions   Big Ten Ch

Isiah Thomas
Ted Kitchel
Chuck Franz
Glen Grunwald
Randy
Bob Knight
Jim Crews   Gerry Hinschef
Wittman
Mike LaFave
Steve Downing
Steve Skocrouki
Tony Brown
Landon Turner
Steve Bouchie

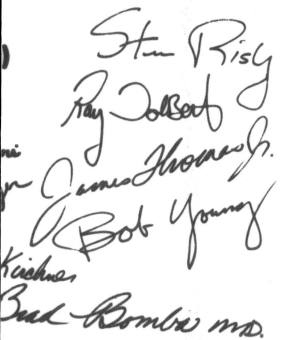

Stan Risly
Ray Tolbert
James Thomas Jr.
Bob Young
Kirchner
Bud Bomba m.d.

11
1980 – 1981

A Sleeping Giant
Awakens

WHEN New Year's Eve ushered in
1981, Indiana had little to celebrate. The
Hoosiers returned from Honolulu and the
Rainbow Classic after dropping two games.
As conference play approached, their
record stood at 7-5.

With the Hoosiers hoping to turn
the season in a positive direction, Michigan
State was their first test in the Big Ten.
Focusing on defense and placing three
players in double figures, IU downed the
Spartans in a low-scoring 55-43 game.

The dazzling shooting performance of Ted Kitchel was the highlight of the next game, against the visiting Illini. The junior forward set the nets on fire, hitting 11 of 13 from the field and was an automatic 18 for 18 at the charity stripe. At game's end, Kitchel had accumulated a career high 40 points and Indiana was victorious, 78-61. The first twelve games of the season, he had averaged ten points per game.

LEFT
Ray Tolbert claims
the fruit of victory.

**Team Roster 1980-1981
(Overall 26-9, Big Ten 14-4,
First in Conference)**

#	Player	Pos.	Year
11	Isiah Thomas	G	So
20	Jim Thomas	G	So
23	Chuck Franz	G	So
24	Randy Wittman	G/F	J
30	Ted Kitchel	F	J
31	Tony Brown	G	So
32	Landon Turner	F/C	J
33	Eric Kirchner	F	S
34	Steve Risley	F	S
40	Glen Grunwald	F	S
42	Craig Bardo	G	F
43	Mike LaFave	F	F
44	Phil Isenbarger	F	S
45	Ray Tolbert	F/C	S
54	Steve Bouchie	F	So

RIGHT
Kitchel's 40
points against
Illinois were a
career high.

ABOVE
Teammates express appreciation after Ted Kitchel's performance against Illinois.

RIGHT
The floor savvy of a young Isiah Thomas led Indiana and brought him All-American status as a sophomore.

The remainder of the Big Ten season brought four losses scattered among twelve wins. Contenders for the conference crown, the Hoosiers claimed it outright for the second straight year with a victory in the last game of the season at Michigan State. Isiah Thomas was named first team All-American, and senior Ray Tolbert received Big Ten Most Valuable Player accolades.

Entering the NCAA Tournament with nine losses, few gave the Hoosiers a serious chance of traveling far along the road to the Final Four. At this point, Indiana put it into overdrive and never looked back.

Maryland was the first victim, as IU clicked on all cylinders. Shooting .651 for the game, hitting 17 of 20 at the line and accumulating only nine turnovers, the Hoosiers buried the Terrapins, 99-64. All Indiana starters finished the game in double digits. The victory gave IU the privilege of playing the next round of Mideast Regional games in familiar territory: Assembly Hall.

Traveling to Bloomington, UAB and coach Gene Bartow found the Hoosiers revving it up and experienced an 87-72 loss before the partisan Indiana crowd. Next on the path to Philadelphia was another home encounter, this time against St. Joseph's College. With Tolbert and Turner teaming up for 14 points each, Jim Thomas stepped in to score 12 when Wittman was injured. The Hoosiers had an outstanding shooting percentage of .686 and easily cruised to victory. With three minutes remaining in the game, the starters gleefully watched from the sidelines as their teammates sealed the deal: Indiana 78, St. Joseph's 46.

The Spectrum played host to Final Four teams Indiana, Louisiana State, Virginia, and North Carolina. Coach Dale Brown and fourth-ranked SEC champion LSU entered the game favored over IU. At the end of the first half, the Tigers were three up on the Hoosiers, 30-27. IU had missed their last ten shots of the half and Isiah Thomas had been saddled with three fouls. The second half was all Indiana, as they went ahead 31-30 on a Landon Turner score.

LEFT
Strong tournament performances from Tolbert and Turner helped IU claim the crown

Turner had a great game, as did Jim Thomas who was called into duty when Isiah collected his fourth foul. With a twenty-point IU lead, all Hoosier players participated in the victory. LSU was held to 49 points, compared to Indiana's 67, vaulting the Hoosiers into the final game.

From Saturday until the morning of the final game, much of the attention was on North Carolina's Dean Smith and IU's Bob Knight. With two proven and respected coaches, the upcoming game presented a matchup of the coaching minds that excited observers.

BELOW
The two Thomases confer on court.

The focus dramatically changed on Monday morning, March 30, 1981. The attempted assassination of President Ronald Reagan outside the Washington Hilton gathered the nation's attention and concern. With a gunshot wound in the chest, the president was rushed to surgery, and Americans were in shock. As the day progressed, reports that President Reagan was responding and recovering well were released. Following surgery, he was reported as saying, "All things being equal, I'd rather be in Philadelphia."

The decision by the NCAA to play the final game that night was reached after hours of deliberation and debate. It was met with opposition, but the game went on. Hoosier players learned of the president's danger from television at the hotel. Sophomore Chuck Franz recalls that the coaching staff did a remarkable job of handling the situation. The team went through the normal game-day routine, with walk-throughs and pregame meals as usual. The idea that the game might not be played was never raised by the coaches.

"We got in the locker room and started getting dressed and started getting ready to go out on the court. Coach Knight comes in and he's just all jacked up—this is before we go out before our first warmup. He says, 'We're going to play the game.' That was the first inkling that we had that there could possibly have been a [postponement]."

North Carolina and Indiana had met in Chapel Hill in December. UNC was victorious. This time, the Tar Heels raced off to a 16-8 lead. The Hoosiers were concerned. Starter Ted Kitchel left the game with three fouls in four minutes, and Jim Thomas came off the bench to make strong contributions. The Hoosiers trailed the entire first half, until junior Randy Wittman stepped up to sink an outside shot from the corner as time expired. It was Indiana's first lead.

Wittman's shot proved the turning point, and after the twenty-minute break, IU increased the lead and took control. The final outcome seemed apparent for much of the second half, as Indiana rolled to claim the title National Champions once again—the second time for Coach Bob Knight, the fourth in Indiana history. Hoosier sophomore Isiah Thomas was named Outstanding Player in the Final Four. Teammates Jim Thomas and Landon Turner joined him on the All-Final Four Team.

The all-night celebration in Bloomington culminated in a joyous gathering at Assembly Hall. Over 10,000 fans were on hand to enthusiastically show their appreciation when the 1981 National Champions arrived around one o'clock Tuesday afternoon. Wearing NCAA Championship hats and victory nets, Hoosier players and fans together savored the moment.

BELOW
The return of the champions!

A Player Remembers

"I had a premonition, about four or five months before that happened, in a dream in which I saw the caption about the *other* Thomas, and it didn't make any sense to me at the time. But after we won the championship, *Sports Illustrated* ran an article, and it talked about *the other Thomas*. When I saw it I thought, 'Oh, that is just like I saw in the dream,' but I could not see the whole part. I only saw part of it.

It was in … November [that] I had it, and it was one of those dreams where it was odd because of the wording, and it stayed with me, but it didn't dawn on me until after we won. Keith Smart, another former player who would win in 1987, said he had a dream sort of like that before it all took place, about the team winning the championship in the Superdome."

—Jim Thomas, on whether the team had a shot at winning the NCAA Tournament and his being named to the Final Four Team
Guard, 1979 – 1983
Final Four Team, 1981
Assistant Coach, 2001 – Present

A Player Remembers

"We were so well prepared every game. Heading into that game, we knew Maryland was a very difficult first-round opponent for us … I mean, they had Buck Williams and Albert King, two future NBA stars. We were going to have to play to the best of our ability. We were so prepared for what they were going to do. We knew every move that they were going to make. And that's true most any game we get into, the way we were prepared by the coaching staff.

It was kind of funny. Lefty Driesell was the coach of Maryland. We were warming up in front of their bench with about five minutes before game time. He knew who Isiah Thomas was, but he didn't even know who Ray Tolbert was, he didn't know Landon. He was asking the other coaches about which one is Tolbert, which one is Turner.

We all heard it. And at that point it was almost like, we're gonna crush these guys."

—Chuck Franz
Guard, 1979 – 1984

12

1981 — 1982

Regrouping

ON July 25, 1981, Landon Turner was paralyzed from spinal injuries suffered in an auto crash on his way to King's Island. The news jolted the Indiana community and brought fans and teammates together in efforts to support the Hoosier center. Turner was a key to the successful turnaround of the 1981 national championship team. Hard work, determination and the development of defensive skills earned Landon a place on the All-Final Four team with outstanding play in Philadelphia.

The next year brought challenge for the Hoosiers. Isiah was lost to the pros; Tolbert, Risley, Grunwald and Isenbarger to graduation. Now the loss of Landon affected the team mentally as well. "It was always because of him that we could get through it the next year," says teammate Chuck Franz.

A season of tough play found Indiana fighting to overcome challenges on and off the court. The end of the year saw Indiana with a respectable 19-10 overall record and a tie for a second-place finish in the Big Ten at 12-6.

LEFT
Freshman Uwe Blab makes his presence known to the Hawkeyes.

RIGHT
Team captain Landon Turner accepts the Indiana Classic trophy from Governor Doc Bowen.

1981-1982 Team Roster (Overall 19-10, Big Ten 12-6, Second in Conference)

#	Player	Pos.	Year
11	Dan Dakich	G	F
20	Jim Thomas	G	J
21	Winston Morgan	G/F	F
23	Chuck Franz	G	J
24	Randy Wittman	F	J
25	Cam Cameron	G	J
30	Ted Kitchel	F	J
31	Tony Brown	G	J
33	Uwe Blab	C	F
42	John Flowers	F	F
43	Mike LaFave	F	So
44	Rick Rowray	F	F
54	Steve Bouchie	F	J

On a lighter note, the home Purdue game was the site of an unusual referee call: a technical foul on the Indiana cheerleaders. Waving the "Go Big Red" flag to the William Tell Overture, the squad failed to notice the time-out was over and remained on the floor . Referee Jim Bain called a technical foul on IU for delay of the game. Coach Bob Knight promptly walked across court and with a smile on his face talked with senior captains Bill Patterson and Sonnie Sicklesmith. Fortunately, the technical was inconsequential, and IU won, 77-55.

A Cheerleader Remembers

"Bill Patterson and I . . . were looking at Coach Knight coming across this court at us and we were thinking, "Oh my gosh, we are in so much trouble!' But we were laughing because it was funny. He comes to [us] because we were the captains, and we had just been in his office a couple of weeks before that. He knew us and was always very kind and respectful and wonderful to us. Honestly, I felt like it was a father scolding his children. He was very nice, and he said, 'You guys are the best group we have ever had. You are wonderful. You support us. You do a great job, but you really need to get your act together.' It was something like that.

The very next game, the manager from the basketball team came across the court during pregame and handed me an 8x10 picture [from] Coach Knight. It said, 'Best wishes, Sonnie. Coach Knight.' I thought that was very special."

—Sonnie Sicklesmith McCauley
Cheerleader Captain, 1982

IU IQ

The starting line-up for the '75-76 season was the same in all 32 games. True or False?

After winning the 1976 NCAA title, the Hoosiers visited which U.S. president in the White House?
a. Richard Nixon
b. Gerald Ford
c. Jimmy Carter
d. Ronald Reagan

Kent Benson was the first player taken in the NBA draft. Who drafted him?
a. Boston
b. Milwaukee
c. Indiana
d. Chicago

In the 1977 Big Ten season, which school had to forfeit two wins to IU?
a. Northwestern
b. Michigan
c. Minnesota
d. Iowa

The leading scorer on the '77-78 team was:
a. Mike Woodson
b. Wayne Radford
c. Ray Tolbert
d. Steve Risley

When Mike Woodson scored 48 points in a game, who was IU playing?
a. Kentucky
b. Purdue
c. Ohio State
d. Illinois

March 29, 1976	December 14, 1977	March 21, 1979	December 18, 1979
IU defeats Michigan, 86-68, to claim national title and complete undefeated season	IU defeats No. 2-ranked Notre Dame, 67-66, at Assembly Hall	In a nail-biter, IU defeats Purdue in New York City to win National Invitational Tournament	Hoosiers defeat Toledo; Mike Woodson scores 19 playing his last game

Which IU player was a member of the 1980 Olympic team?

The Big Ten 1980 MVP was:
a. Isiah Thomas
b. Ray Tolbert
c. Mike Woodson
d. Ted Kitchel

Which Indiana player was named MVP of the Indiana Classic in 1980?
a. Randy Wittman
b. Isiah Thomas
c. Ray Tolbert
d. Landon Turner

In '80-81, Isiah Thomas had ___ more assists than all other IU players.
a. 90
b. 100
c. 110
d. 120

Of these players on the '80-81 team, who played for IU more than two years?
a. Isiah Thomas
b. Mike LaFave
c. Chuck Franz
d. Craig Bardo

In 1982, he was the tallest player in IU history.

The player who led the '81-82 Hoosiers in both rebounding and assists was:
a. Ted Kitchel
b. Randy Wittman
c. Jim Thomas
d. Uwe Blab

Answers: True; b. Gerald Ford; b. Milwaukee; c. Minnesota; a. Mike Woodson (577 pts); d. Illinois; Isiah Thomas; c. Mike Woodson d. Landon Turner; d.120 (He had 197/ Wittman and J. Thomas had 77); c. Chuck Franz; Uwe Blab; c. Jim Thomas (181 rebounds/103 assists)

February 14, 1980	January 10, 1981	March 30, 1981	January 31, 1982
Mike Woodson marks his return to play by hitting his first three shots as the Hoosiers defeat Iowa 66-55	Ted Kitchel hits 18 of 18 free throws and scores 40 against Illinois in Bloomington	President Ronald Reagan is shot; Indiana Hoosiers are four-time National Champions after defeating North Carolina	Cheerleaders receive a delay of game technical foul at Assembly Hall during Purdue game

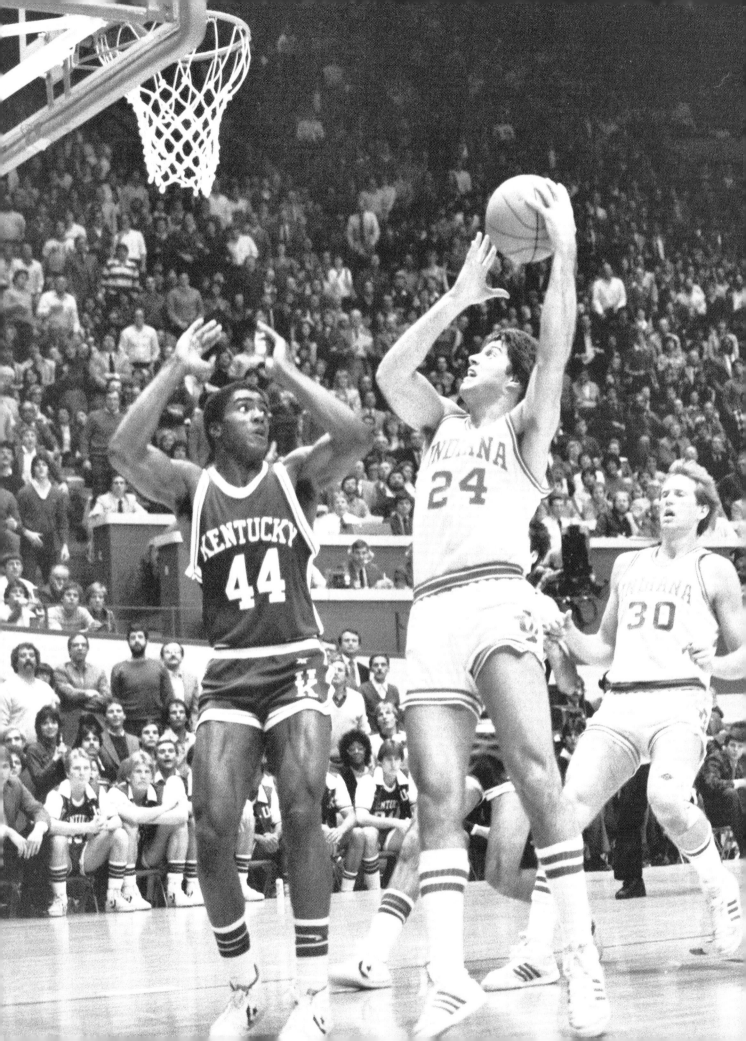

13

1982 – 1983

Year of the Big Ten Banner

THE phrase *older and wiser* doesn't seem to fit a group of 21-22-year-old guys. But it certainly was an apt description of the five senior players who led the Indiana squad in 1982–1983. When Wittman, Kitchel, J. Thomas, Bouchie and Brown stepped off the court for the last time, they could claim 114 victories, three Big Ten titles, an NIT crown and an NCAA Championship.

Perhaps the most meaningful of the Big Ten crowns was earned their senior year. Blitzing into the season with a 10-0 record which included a three-point victory over No. 2-ranked Kentucky, IU sat atop the polls for two weeks. The Big Ten season opener and loss against Ohio State brought Hoosier fans back to earth. The team recovered quickly and moved on to establish a 10-3 Big Ten record and a two-game lead with less than three weeks remaining in the season.

LEFT
Randy Wittman played in more games than any other Hoosier. His 133 games is still the Indiana record.

Ann Arbor was the site of Ted Kitchel's last play as an Indiana Hoosier. Six minutes into the first half, the fifth-year senior left the game and soon required back surgery. With a major offensive weapon missing, the team fell to Michigan and then lost the next game at Michigan State. The title hopes, strong a week before, were now in jeopardy.

With three home games to go, rival Purdue rolled into Assembly Hall. The Boilers and Iowa were now tied with IU for the Big Ten lead. One week after back surgery, the surprise appearance of Kitchel seconds before the game ignited the already fired-up home fans. Final score: Indiana 64, Purdue 41. Illinois and Ohio State followed with a similar fate. On an emotional Senior Day, Indiana claimed a special Big Ten title.

Senior Randy Wittman was named All-American and Big Ten MVP. An outstanding year closed with an overall record of 24-6 and Big Ten mark of 13-5.

ABOVE
The senior from Washington, Indiana successfully used his hook shot during his four years at IU.

A Coach Speaks

W e've always kinda reserved banners in here for things that happened on a national level. We're going to break from that tradition a little bit. Because everybody had a big part in this, when you come in here next fall, down there [pointing to the north end of Assembly Hall] there will be a banner that says '1983 Big Ten Champions.' Remember when you see it, that's a banner that belongs to every one of you."

—Bob Knight, March 12, 1983
Indiana Head Coach, 1971 – 2000

**Team Roster
(Overall 24-6, Big Ten 13-5,
First in Conference)**

#	Player	Pos.	Year
11	Dan Dakich	G	So
20	Jim Thomas	G	S
21	Winston Morgan	G/F	So
22	Stew Robinson	G	F
23	Chuck Franz	G	S
24	Randy Wittman	G/F	S
25	Cam Cameron	G	S
30	Ted Kitchel	F	S
31	Tony Brown	G	S
33	Uwe Blab	C	So
40	Tracy Foster	F	F
41	Mike Giomi	F	F
42	John Flowers	F/C	So
54	Steve Bouchie	F	S

RIGHT
Guard Tony Brown was the
assist leader for the '82-83
team with 116.

14

1983 – 1984,
1984 – 1985,
1985 – 1986

Building
for the Future

A roller coaster ride describes the next three
years of Indiana basketball. With lots of highs and
lows, a new group of talented players experienced
lean times and struggles, which built character and
insight that served them well in 1987.

The '83-84 season closed at a very respectable 22-9 with a third-place conference finish.
Along the way, four freshmen, Steve Alford, Marty
Simmons, Daryl Thomas and Todd Meier, learned
some valuable lessons.

LEFT
Steve Alford receives
national attention as
he is interviewed by
Al McGuire.

After experiencing a rare homecourt loss to Purdue, Coach Knight was disgusted with the effort and the team. The next practice day, the home locker room was locked and off limits and the team banished to the visitor's locker room. The following day, both locker rooms were closed and the players dressed in the hallway. Knight declared that he was not coaching this team and directed senior Chuck Franz to take over.

With a Thursday game at Michigan State coming up, Franz was told to make all necessary travel arrangements. The coaching staff was either not present at practices or would not speak to the team. The team had to prepare themselves for the game: film review, practices, pregame. Minutes before game time, Coach Knight and athletic director Ralph Floyd entered the locker room for the first time in days and preceded the team onto the court (a rarity in Knight's days). Once the game was underway, life returned to normal. Today Franz says the larger lesson learned was one consistently taught by Coach Knight: It doesn't matter what the other team does; what matters is what you do. Indiana won the game in overtime.

The highlight of the season occurred when the Hoosiers took on No. 1-ranked North Carolina in the NCAA Regional. With Sam Perkins, Brad Daugherty, and Michael Jordan, UNC was the favorite team of the nation and was expected to fly to a national title. In a masterful job of motivation and preparation, Bob Knight and team shocked the Tar Heels and oddsmakers by defeating UNC, 72-68 . The lesson that week was: If you will listen to me and do what I set up, we will beat North Carolina. Victory = lesson learned.

Team Roster 1983-1984
(Overall 22-9, Big Ten 13-5,
Third in Conference)

#	Player	Pos.	Year
11	Dan Dakich	G	J
12	Steve Alford	G	F
21	Winston Morgan	G/F	J
22	Stew Robinson	G	So
23	Chuck Franz	G	S
24	Daryl Thomas	G/F	F
25	Cam Cameron	G	S
30	Todd Meier	F	F
33	Uwe Blab	C	J
40	Tracy Foster	F	So
41	Mike Giomi	F	So
50	Marty Simmons	F	F
52	Courtney Witte	F	J

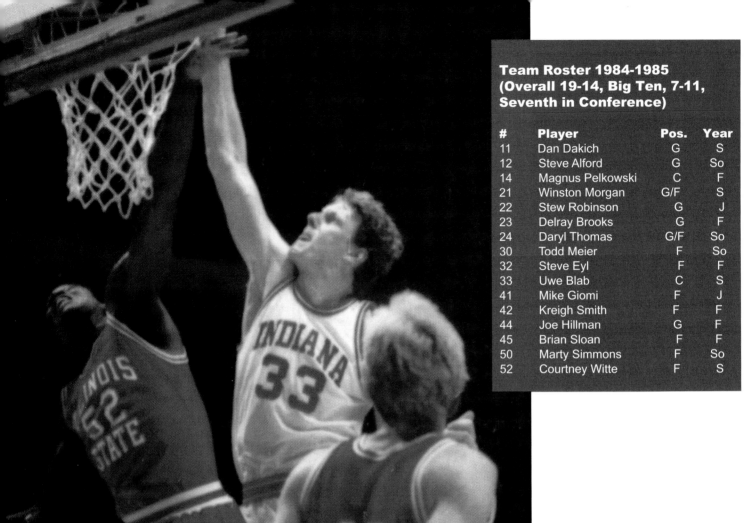

**Team Roster 1984-1985
(Overall 19-14, Big Ten, 7-11,
Seventh in Conference)**

#	Player	Pos.	Year
11	Dan Dakich	G	S
12	Steve Alford	G	So
14	Magnus Pelkowski	C	F
21	Winston Morgan	G/F	S
22	Stew Robinson	G	J
23	Delray Brooks	G	F
24	Daryl Thomas	G/F	So
30	Todd Meier	F	So
32	Steve Eyl	F	F
33	Uwe Blab	C	S
41	Mike Giomi	F	J
42	Kreigh Smith	F	F
44	Joe Hillman	G	F
45	Brian Sloan	F	F
50	Marty Simmons	F	So
52	Courtney Witte	F	S

RIGHT
In 1985, Blab was named an
Academic All-American.

The '84–85 season is one of dubious distinction. With seven wins against eleven losses, Indiana finished an uncharacteristic seventh place in the Big Ten. Never before had Assembly Hall supporters witnessed seven home losses in one season.

The most remembered event of the year is one that found its way into the memory banks of America. Disagreeing with two foul calls on Indiana in a home game against Purdue, Knight received a technical foul. He then grabbed a sideline chair and threw it spinning across the court while Boiler Steve Reid stood at the foul line. "The Chair Incident" resulted in his instant ejection from the game and an additional one-game suspension.

Not invited to the big dance, the Hoosiers did end the season on an up note with a respectable showing in the National Invitational Tournament. After winning their first four NIT challenges and making it to the final game in New York, Indiana lost 62-65 to UCLA, which featured forward Reggie Miller.

The summer months were spent traveling to Canada, Japan, China, Yugoslavia and Finland, playing basketball and representing the U.S. in the Kirin World Basketball Championships. When the squad returned in the fall, there was something to prove as they looked to rebound from the previous season. Junior Daryl Thomas showed great improvement and was moved into the center position.

Good shooting became a trademark of the '85-86 Hoosiers as they finished the season hitting .537 percent. A vastly improved conference record of 13-5 put IU close to attaining another Big Ten title. A loss to Michigan in the last game of the season gave the title to the Wolverines.

This season, chronicled in John Feinstein's *A Season on the Brink,* featured a turn-around that pointed the team in the right direction for the future.

LEFT
Indiana's Mr. Basketball of '83, Steve Alford earned his place in IU history.

93

A Fan's Perspective

"Since I was two years old, Assembly Hall was somewhat of a second home as my parents, no exaggeration, took me to every home game. Of all the memories in Assembly Hall, none are greater than the dream it let me live when I was just a little kid. After every game I was allowed to walk down those steep steps, step onto the court with my little basketball, and live a fantasy. I would mimic the game just watched, mimic the games played earlier in the year, or dream the ultimate dream of wearing those red and white candy-striped pants and donning the Indiana jersey. When I was on that floor, I wasn't just an IU fan; I was part of the game, part of the history, part of tradition."

—Josh Tolliver
Student 1998 – 2002

ABOVE
Five-year-old Josh Tolliver
living the dream.

A Player Remembers

"We really believed that if we followed the game plan, we would win. And the only question was, 'Who was going to guard Jordan?' Because it was either going to be Stew Robinson, Danny Dakich or myself. It was going to be one of the three of us. And we'd all practiced that way. It didn't matter who it was. We all felt, somebody is going to have to do this in the game.

The game plan was, basically, let him get the ball. Most people try to take the ball away from him, denying it. . . . [But] when you deny him the ball, he would run to the basket. They'd throw it up there. He could jump higher than you and he'd dunk it. So the game plan was let him catch it.

That's totally against what some people think about IU defense, and that's what a great coach Coach Knight is. Through looking at films, he was able to really mess up somebody's offense just by doing one simple thing."

—Chuck Franz
Guard, 1979 – 1984

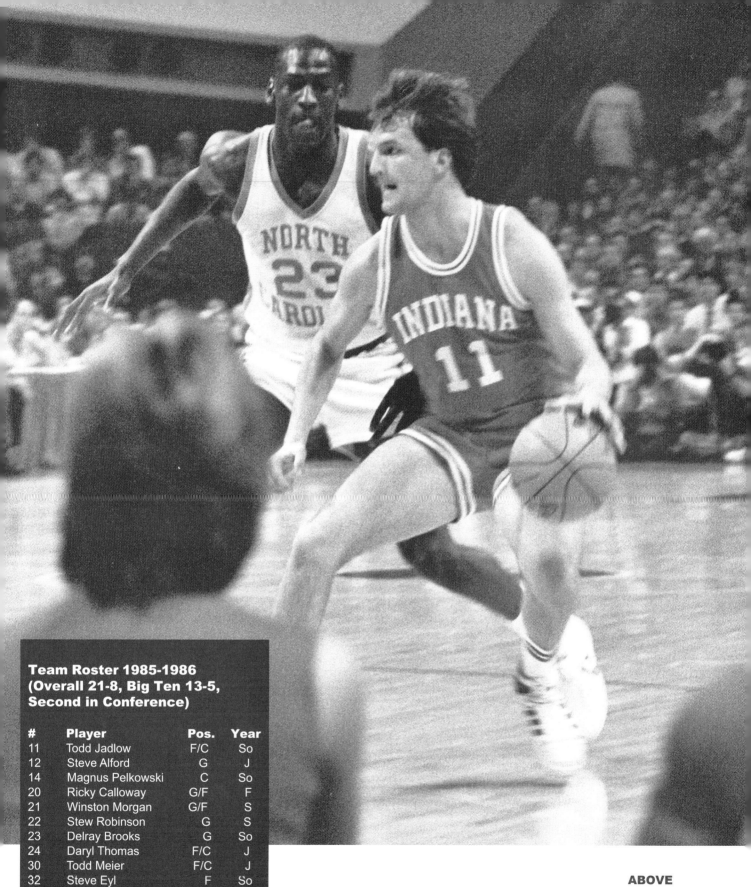

**Team Roster 1985-1986
(Overall 21-8, Big Ten 13-5,
Second in Conference)**

#	Player	Pos.	Year
11	Todd Jadlow	F/C	So
12	Steve Alford	G	J
14	Magnus Pelkowski	C	So
20	Ricky Calloway	G/F	F
21	Winston Morgan	G/F	S
22	Stew Robinson	G	S
23	Delray Brooks	G	So
24	Daryl Thomas	F/C	J
30	Todd Meier	F/C	J
32	Steve Eyl	F	So
34	Andre Harris	F	J
35	Jeff Oliphant	G	F
42	Kreigh Smith	F	So
44	Joe Hillman	G	So
45	Brian Sloan	F/C	So
52	Courtney Witte	F	S

ABOVE

Following Coach Knight's game plan, IU upsets UNC and Michael Jordan. When Dan Dakich was told he would guard Jordan, he promptly returned to his hotel room and threw up.

15
1986 – 1987
"The Shot"

UNLIKE recent years, the season kicked off with the hint of promise in the air. Seniors Alford, Meier and Thomas had spent the last three years in the trenches gaining experience and developing their talent. Joined by two junior college transfers, Keith Smart and Dean Garrett, and supported by a strong cast that included returning Rick Calloway, last year's Big Ten Freshman of the Year, Indiana looked like a true contender. The Hoosiers began play ranked No. 3 in the AP poll.

After three wins, the first loss came at Vanderbilt and established a pattern for the rest of the season. The four losses of the year all came on away courts. As usual, Indiana Classic and Hoosier Classic titles were awarded to IU in December.

The always anticipated clashes with intrastate rival Purdue were especially hyped in the '86-87 season. Both teams were nationally ranked in the top ten on each encounter. The first meeting in Bloomington featured 31 points by Alford and double figures by three teammates as IU prevailed 88-77. A month later Purdue turned the table on the Hoosiers at Mackey Arena.

A truly memorable game in the annals of Indiana basketball took place on February 16, 1987 in Madison, Wisconsin. In an ESPN late game with a 9:42 P.M. tipoff, the Badgers took the Hoosiers into overtime with a 62-62 tie. IU maintained a slim lead much of the overtime, but a determined Wisconsin club tied it at 70-70 and Indiana could not convert on three opportunities as time again expired.

Second overtime. With 28 seconds remaining, IU went ahead 79-76 when Calloway scored on a layup. Despite a defense primed for the three-point shot, Wisconsin's Ripley hit from beyond the arch with eight seconds showing on the clock. Alford's shot at the buzzer missed and a third overtime ensued.

Wisconsin was ahead 85-84 with 37 seconds left. Keith Smart sank two pressure free throws to make it a one-point deficit. At last, down to three seconds, a rebound basket by Dean Garrett made the weary Hoosiers the 86-85 winners. This win went into the record books as the first and only triple overtime game in the history of Indiana basketball.

After two losses at Purdue and Illinois, a pressure-filled Senior Day pitted IU against OSU. The Hoosiers were victorious and needed an obliging Michigan's defeat of Purdue to give Indiana a share of the Big Ten Crown.

The NCAA Tournament pairings pleased the Indiana faithful. Seeded No. 1 in the Midwest Regional, IU was slotted to play first-round games in the Indianapolis Hoosier Dome. A record crowd of 34,000-plus and a sea of red greeted the white-jerseyed team, which easily downed Fairfield, 92-58.

Indiana helped themselves by shooting .544. Auburn initially provided a stronger challenge and got the attention of all in the Dome when they posted a 24-10 early lead. By focusing on defense and shooting .603 from the field, IU marched on with a 107-90 win.

Cincinnati hosted the Regional Semifinal and Final games. The media spent much of the week examining the coaching matchup of former Army player Mike Krzyzewski of Duke and his ex-coach, Bob Knight.

RIGHT
Alford was a two-time All-American, 1986 and 1987.

Duke, with standouts Ferry, Amaker and Strickland, led midway through the first half 31-24, but a surge by IU took them into the break with a ten-point 49-39 lead. The Dukies closed the lead to two but could not catch the Hoosiers. Rick Calloway played well in front of the hometown crowd and scored 21 to help ensure the 88-82 win.

The Sunday game was a heart stopper. Louisiana State and coach Dale Brown were formidable foes. After a see-saw first half, the Tigers forged ahead 63-51. Indiana fought back and closed the gap to 75-68. Scratching and clawing to stay in the game, the scoreboard showed 0:26, LSU 76-75 with a Tiger at the line. The free throw missed, and Daryl Thomas rebounded. With Alford well defended, Daryl Thomas's shot fell short. Calloway flew in to grab the ball and put it through the net with six seconds remaining. Indiana won 77-76 and bedlam erupted in the arena and the living rooms of Indiana loyalists.

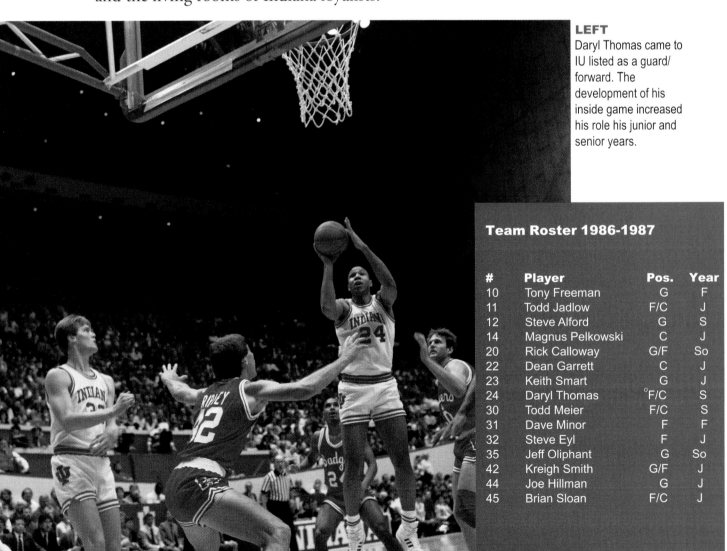

LEFT
Daryl Thomas came to IU listed as a guard/ forward. The development of his inside game increased his role his junior and senior years.

Team Roster 1986-1987

#	Player	Pos.	Year
10	Tony Freeman	G	F
11	Todd Jadlow	F/C	J
12	Steve Alford	G	S
14	Magnus Pelkowski	C	J
20	Rick Calloway	G/F	So
22	Dean Garrett	C	J
23	Keith Smart	G	J
24	Daryl Thomas	°F/C	S
30	Todd Meier	F/C	S
31	Dave Minor	F	F
32	Steve Eyl	F	J
35	Jeff Oliphant	G	So
42	Kreigh Smith	G/F	J
44	Joe Hillman	G	J
45	Brian Sloan	F/C	J

A trip to New Orleans and the Superdome awaited the Final Four-bound Hoosiers. The favored and No. 1-ranked University of Nevada-Las Vegas were the next gigantic task. Sporting a 37-1 record and a high-powered offense, the Running Rebels faced No. 2-ranked Indiana with confidence. In an exciting, fast-paced game that featured lead changes and great basketball, IU upset UNLV 97-93 in front of crowd of 64,959.

One challenge remained.

Film makers choose I.U. over Oscars

The Associated Press

ALTHOUGH *HOOSIERS* put some of the Oscar spotlight on Indiana, all eyes here, it seems, were focused on Hoosiers of another sort—the ones playing a championship basketball game, just like in the movie.

Even the producers, David Anspaugh and Angelo Pizzo, chose to stay home Monday night and watch their alma mater, Indiana University, play Syracuse in the NCAA championship.

"If it wasn't for Indiana basketball, I'd never have written *Hoosiers*. So that's what comes first," said Pizzo, whose movie was nominated for two Oscars but came up short.

Pizzo, who graduated in 1971, said he and Anspaugh turned on two television sets Monday night and watched the Academy Awards and the game at Anspaugh's Los Angeles home.

Pizzo, 38, said they originally planned to attend the Oscars and take two-inch-screen TVs. He said, however, he didn't want to risk the televisions not working.

"We decided we would go crazy sitting in the auditorium not knowing what was happening with IU So we decided to forego our tickets to watch the game," he said.

Two words, "The Shot," produce a smile and an adrenaline rush for any Hoosier fan. "The Shot" brings feelings of exhilaration. "The Shot" is one of the pinnacle moments in over one hundred years of Indiana basketball.

Down 72-73 to the Syracuse Orangemen in the final game of the 1987 NCAA Tournament, Keith Smart took a pass from Daryl Thomas and with four seconds in the game, lofted a 16-foot jumper that hit nothing but net.

Four Hoosier players did all the scoring for IU. Alford had 23, Smart 21, Thomas 20 and Garrett 10. Down the stretch, the huge plays came from #23.

On March 31st, 1987, "The Shot" claimed its place in Hoosier folklore forever.

A Player Remembers

"I thought the game was over for me, and then Coach asked me if I was ready to play. Syracuse had made a big run and gotten themselves back into the game, and I said, 'Yes, I am ready to play.' He said, 'Well, you have a couple of minutes to go in and play. If you haven't done anything in a couple of minutes, I am taking you out and I can't use you.' So I figured being at home in Baton Rouge where I am from, with all the family there, I better do something to stay on the floor. I got in there and started playing and things started to open up and I started to make plays.

The strangest thing was that I was able to go back into the game and I didn't see anyone in the arena. Strange as it may sound, I didn't see anyone on the floor. I was in the arena on the floor by myself playing. And I played as if I was outside playing somewhere. I had all the time in the world to make the right pass. All the time in the world to make the right shot, the right decision. It was like athletes talk about—being in the zone.

You don't really ever get to that place again, but I guess that's because I felt like I was playing by myself. I didn't hear anything else again until the final shot when I heard this explosion of noise, and that kind of brought me back to reality."

—Keith Smart
Guard, 1987 – 1988
NCAA Tournament MVP, 1987

ABOVE
Coach Knight and team present
President Reagan with gifts during
their meeting at the White House.

A Fan's Perspective

W e watched the IU victory over UNLV with three other couples, all IU grads. The next day, Sunday, over breakfast, we decided to go to New Orleans, and two hours later we were on the road. Two couples driving in a midsize car, picked up the fifth person in Memphis, then picked up the sixth person at the New Orleans airport Monday morning. We [bought] scalped tickets for $100 and couldn't believe we would spend sooo much money to watch a basketball game. With only 38 seconds to go Syracuse was at the foul line leading 73-70, while two obnoxious Syracuse fans were behind us celebrating an almost certain victory. All I could think about was "Why had I driven 12 hours to New Orleans to watch Indiana lose so we could drive another 12 hours back home tomorrow!?!' Who would have guessed that 38 seconds and two Keith Smart field goals later we would be the obnoxious fans celebrating Indiana's victory!

We celebrated with the team on Bourbon Street, left the next morning (all six of us) and drove back to Indianapolis in a mid-size car. We got home at 6:00 A.M. We watched the video of the game, I bet ten times, and each and every time it was exciting. Then to find ourselves in 'The Last Shot' picture of Keith Smart was truly the icing on the cake for us "

—John Rademaker
Student, 1967 – 1971

16
1987 – 1988,
1988 – 1989

The Sequel: Reality / Rebound

AT a New Orleans postgame victory rally following Indiana's defeat of UNLV, an announcement that Marion High School had captured the Indiana High School Basketball championship brought a loud round of cheers from Hoosier fans. The promise of the arrival of Co-Mr. Basketballs Jay Edwards and Lyndon Jones on future rosters carried with it the hope of extending the successful tradition and of prolonging the euphoria of the moment.

The new season got off to a decent start at 8-2. Shock set in, however, when five games into Big Ten, Indiana found itself 1-4 with losses to Iowa, Northwestern, Michigan State and Michigan. In a year when the conference was exceptionally strong, four losses in January made a repeat title seem an insurmountable task. Moving to a three-guard lineup of Joe Hillman, Lyndon Jones and Jay Edwards brought five straight victories highlighted by a win over the visiting Boilermakers. Dean Garrett was the hero with 31 points and the go-ahead basket. The lineup change meant less playing time for Smart and Calloway. The Big Ten season ended with an 11-7 record and a fifth-place standing. Jay Edwards led the conference in three-point and free-throw shooting percentage and was named the Big Ten Freshman of the Year.

LEFT
Jay's buzzer-beater
lifted the Hoosiers over
Michigan 76-75.

Expected to finish in the middle of the pack, the '88-89 Hoosiers brought smiles and the Big Ten trophy back to Bloomington.

The year began with a discouraging start, however. In the first six games the IU "D" looked uncharacteristically weak and allowed Syracuse, North Carolina and Louisville to score 100-plus points. The result was a lineup change once again, featuring the trio of Hillman, Edwards and Jones. The first game of the change was a loss to Notre Dame, but thirteen consecutive victories followed. Joining the squad was newcomer Eric Anderson at forward. Todd Jadlow provided support when he scored 32 points against ninth-ranked Iowa.

In a year that began with Michigan, Illinois and Iowa ranked among the top ten teams in the nation, Indiana surprised them all and snatched the title, the ninth for Coach Knight. Along the way they provided supreme entertainment for fans with unbelievable last-second shots in at least three games.

ABOVE
Senior Dean Garrett was the leading scorer and rebounder on the '87-88 squad.

\#	Player	Pos.	Year
3	Jay Edwards	G/F	F
4	Lyndon Jones	G	F
10	Mark Robinson	F	J
11	Todd Jadlow	F/C	J
14	Magnus Pelkowski	C	J
20	Rick Calloway	G/F	J
22	Dean Garrett	C	S
23	Keith Smart	G	S
31	Dave Minor	F	So
32	Steve Eyl	F	S
35	Jeff Oliphant	G	So
42	Kreigh Smith	G/F	J
44	Joe Hillman	G	J
45	Brian Sloan	F/C	J

Team Roster 1987-1988 (Overall 19-10, Big Ten 11-7, Fifth in Conference)

The most remembered was the Sunday afternoon Assembly Hall clash with Michigan. With a national television audience watching a close game to the end, Jay Edwards hit his first three-pointer of the day. The buzzer sounded while the ball was in the air and because the ball left Edwards's hands with a fraction of a second remaining, the referee ruled the shot good. The home crowd erupted, and another thrilling moment was stored in the memory book of fans.

A Broadcaster Remembers

"As far as great shots, Keith Smart's shot, without question, is probably the most indelible in anybody's memory.

But Jay Edwards hit some of the most miraculous shots I've ever seen hit in three straight home games. He did it against Purdue, beating the archrival Boilermakers with a last-second, 15-foot baseline shot. In the very next game he stunned Michigan with a shot as time ran out.

IU then played three road games before coming home to meet Illinois. Incredibly, the game again came down to the wire and Edwards *again* buried almost the same baseline bomb to give Indiana apparent victory. But this time there were a couple seconds left on the clock. After time out, the Illini's Nick Anderson took a half-court pass and launched a 35-foot shot that went in to stun the Hoosiers.

Still, those three shots by Jay Edwards are among the most amazing I've ever seen."

—Don Fischer
Indiana Sportscaster of the Year on 22 occasions

RIGHT
1989 Big Ten Freshman of the Year, Eric Anderson, scores two.

Team Roster 1988-1989 (Overall 27-8, Big Ten 15-3, First in Conference)			
#	Player	Pos.	Year
3	Jay Edwards	G/F	So
4	Lyndon Jones	G	So
5	Chuckie White	F	J
10	Mark Robinson	F	J
11	Todd Jadlow	F/C	S
14	Magnus Pelkowski	C	S
21	Mike D'Aloisio	G	S
23	Jamal Meeks	G	F
24	Matt Nover	F	F
32	Eric Anderson	F	F
35	Jeff Oliphant	G	J
42	Kreigh Smith	G/F	3
44	Joe Hillman	G	S
45	Brian Sloan	F/C	S

17

1989 – 1990,
1990 – 1991

A Fabulous Freshman Invasion
Brings Sophomore Success

THE 1989-1990 Hoosier roster listed one senior, one junior, two sophomores and eight freshmen. Youth brings hope and promise for the future. Youth brings inexperience and inconsistency. This group of young men brought more than four years of excitement and glory to Indiana basketball.

Bob Knight's youngest squad ever took to the hardwood and experienced instant success by starting 10-0. Then the realities of Big Ten play hit and sent the novices on a route of ups and downs. Along the way, glimpses of potential and brilliant play surfaced. A colossal comeback against No. 5-ranked Michigan sent Assembly Hall fans into a frenzy when IU grabbed a 69-67 victory. A disappointing seventh-place finish in the conference provided thought for the summer and motivation for next year.

LEFT
Rick Calloway, Tony Freeman, and Kreigh Smith spend some down time in the locker room. Each locker carries the nameplate of its former players. The tradition lives on . . .

Freshmen Calbert Cheaney, Greg Graham, Pat Graham, Chris Reynolds, Chris Lawson, Todd Leary, and redshirt Matt Nover were given enormous amounts of playing time throughout the year. Year-end statistics show freshmen and sophomores as the top five scorers of the season. Funderburke, the recruit receiving the most attention upon arrival at IU, departed after his first semester.

A year of collegiate play and maturity paid benefits for the still young '90-91 Indiana team. Two wins and a loss to Syracuse in the Maui Classic initiated the new season. Returning home, the Hoosiers amassed fourteen consecutive victories to establish themselves as contenders on the national scene.

Joined by the much-talked-about Hoosier high school sensation Damon Bailey, IU lost two games to Ohio State, giving them first place with few conference games remaining. Another five-game win streak combined with an OSU loss gave Indiana a share of the Big Ten crown, the tenth title in the Assembly Hall era.

Freshman Bailey proved deserving of his reputation and scored 32 points in the away loss to the Buckeyes. Damon was named Big Ten Freshman of the Year. The team ended the year shooting .534 percent, the second highest in IU history. A strong 29-5 record was an indicator of improvement and success.

LEFT
Three seasons in a row Jamal Meeks dished out the most assists.

**Team Roster 1989-1990
(Overall 18-11, Big Ten 8-10,
Seventh in Conference)**

#	Player	Pos.	Year
4	Lyndon Jones	G	J
10	Mark Robinson	F	S
20	Greg Graham	G	F
21	Chris Reynolds	G	F
23	Jamal Meeks	G	So
24	Matt Nover	F	F
30	Todd Leary	G	F
32	Eric Anderson	F	So
33	Pat Graham	G	F
34	Lawrence Funderburke	F	F
35	Jeff Oliphant	G	S
40	Calbert Cheaney	G/F	F
54	Chris Lawson	F/C	F

A Player Remembers

"Before going to IU, I read a little blurb on the back page of *The Star* one day. It said Calbert Cheaney signed with Indiana. I had never heard of Calbert Cheaney. I didn't know anything about it. It said he was from Evansville. I didn't know anything about him, but obviously he turned out to be something pretty special. He did that just based on hard work.

Coming in there, he wasn't near the player he was when he left there. It was just all hard work. Calbert was the guy who everyone says, 'Who's the best player you ever played with or against?' I say Calbert in both instances, because I played against him every day in practice and played with him in the games. He worked harder than anyone on every possession, and that was what made him the great player that he was. Him being the best player and working the hardest is probably why we were as successful as we were."

—Todd Leary
Guard, 1989 – 1994
Indiana University Basketball Broadcaster

LEFT
As a freshman Calbert Cheaney led Indiana in scoring.

**Team Roster 1990–1991
(Overall 29-5, Big Ten 15-3,
Tied for First in Conference)**

#	Player	Pos.	Year
4	Lyndon Jones	G	S
20	Greg Graham	G	So
21	Chris Reynolds	G	So
22	Damon Bailey	G	F
23	Jamal Meeks	G	J
24	Matt Nover	F	So
25	Pat Knight	F	F
30	Todd Leary	G	So
32	Eric Anderson	F	J
33	Pat Graham	G	So
40	Calbert Cheaney	G/F	So
54	Chris Lawson	F/C	So

## 18

1991 – 1992

Ride to the
Final Four

THE ingredients for a stellar season were all present: ten returning lettermen, a first team All-American player, the Big Ten Freshman of the Year, a Hall of Fame coach. Would they blend together to produce a team capable of adding a sixth championship banner to Assembly Hall? They came close!

In a year when the Hoosiers won by 30 or more points on ten occasions and beat Purdue 106-65 in the first go-round, fans were hopeful. Indiana was ranked in the top 10 for sixteen weeks of the season. The Sunday game at Ohio State when the Hoosiers defeated the Buckeyes on national TV was one of many highlights of the regular season. Cheaney tallied 28 points in the exciting effort.

TOP TEN REASONS [IU] WINS
1. CEREBRAL REVERSAL
2. BOILERMAKERS LOSE IN N.I.T.
3. BOBBY DIDN'T MOVE TO NEW MEXICO
4. WE CONQUERED THE SHAQ ATTACK
5. RIO GRANDE RIVER NOT AS DEEP AS BOISE RIVER
6. ASSISTANT COACHES DIDN'T SCALP TICKETS
7. WE HAD SECOND HELPINGS OF BUCKEYE PIE
8. NO DISTRACTING BANQUETS
9. WE THOUGHT DON MACLEAN WAS A SINGER
10. N.A.A.C.P. DOESN'T VOTE IN A.P. POLL

The regular season ended with two losses in the last three games and resulted in a second-place finish in the Big Ten and a No. 2 seed in the West Regional of the NCAA Tournament. The team and entourage traveled over 1,800 miles to Boise, Idaho for the first-round games against Eastern Illinois. A 94-55 victory meant a clash with LSU and powerful Shaquille O'Neal. The Hoosiers took the lead with 5:10 left in the first half and never again fell behind. LSU made a surge in the beginning of the second half, but IU played smart and advanced to the Regionals.

"The Pit" in Albuquerque was good to Indiana. Excellent second-half play hoisted the Hoosiers over Florida State, 85-74, in a Friday night game. Sunday brought a meeting with UCLA. IU had lost to the Bruins by 15 in the opening game of the season. Now the stakes were higher: a trip to the Final Four. Teammate Todd Leary recalls the superb performances of Eric Anderson and Calbert Cheaney. "I remember Eric Anderson and Calbert Cheaney just both looking like they said to themselves, we are not losing. I don't care what happens. If I've got to make the toughest shot in the world, I am going to make it. I can remember Eric Anderson knocking down some really, really tough shots. I think that was one of Calbert's better games." Final score, Hoosiers 106, Bruins 79.

March Madness and the privilege of participating in the Final Four creates a week of pregame hype and excitement incomparable to any other event. In Bob Knight's tenure at IU, this was the fifth time Indiana advanced to the Final Four.

With Duke the Hoosiers' Metrodome opponent, the focus once again turned to the relationship between the Indiana coach and former Army player slash Indiana graduate assistant of 1975, Mike Krzyzewski. Coach K's Blue Devils came out on top, but not before IU and Todd Leary, in particular, made it exciting. Ahead by twelve points at one point in the first period, the Hoosiers went into halftime a five-point leader, 42-37. Duke took over in the second half, and when four starters fouled out (Bailey, Henderson, G. Graham, Cheaney), Todd Leary entered the game with 1:14 remaining and IU down 73-64.

BELOW
In his four years at IU, Matt Nover grabbed 535 rebounds and blocked 66 shots.

**Team Roster 1991-1992
(Overall 27-7, Big Ten 14-4,
Second in Conference)**

#	Player	Pos.	Year
20	Greg Graham	G	J
21	Chris Reynolds	G	J
22	Damon Bailey	G	So
23	Jamal Meeks	G	S
24	Matt Nover	F/C	J
25	Pat Knight	F	So
30	Todd Leary	G	So
32	Eric Anderson	F	S
33	Pat Graham	G	J
34	Brian Evans	F	F
40	Calbert Cheaney	F	J
44	Alan Henderson	F/C	F
50	Todd Lindeman	C	F

LEFT
Sophomore Todd Leary entered the NCAA Duke game and scored an incredible three threes within 22 seconds.'

OPPOSITE LOWER RIGHT
Following the Regional victory, a kind Calbert Cheaney takes time to talk to fan Chad Tolliver back home in Indiana.

An amazing 22 seconds followed. At 0:49, seconds after coming off the bench, Leary hit a three-pointer. Duke followed with two free throws. At 0:40 on the clock, Leary hit another three. Another two free throws were made by Duke. A third time, Todd Leary sank a three with 27 seconds remaining. "Oh my goodness! This is legendary," exclaimed CBS announcer Billy Packer. Jim Nance joined in, " This is *Hoosiers*. This is the movie coming to life!"

Not quite enough to bring IU back. Duke prevailed 81-78. The year of the journey to Minneapolis would not be forgotten. Nor would three threes in 22 seconds.

A Player Remembers

"One of the favorite memories is just the support that the whole program received from the city and from the state. You know, just how much they loved us and Coach Knight and everything Indiana basketball represented. It was just great to be a part of that … I will never forget coming back from the Final Four. Getting off the airplane and the whole place was just filled with people. We had just a crowd of people out there, and it was loud just like you were inside of a stadium. They were all lined up and just crowded on the airport all the way to the bus. There was a caravan of cars all on the street and lining the highways from the airport all the way to the stadium.

We got out at the stadium and walked into Assembly Hall. I mean it was thousands and thousands of people out there just cheering for us. When we walked in, they were trying to take our Final Four hats off our heads. I mean it was just a great experience. That was what we went to Indiana for."

—Alan Henderson
Forward/Center, 1992 – 1995
All-American, 1995

A Fan Remembers

"After watching the Hoosiers defeat UCLA, I was pumped. I grabbed the IU flag that was hanging outside the front door and began running up and down our street waving the flag with excitement. I remembered being in Cincinnati in 1987 when we beat LSU to advance to the Final Four and wished I could have been in Albuquerque with my parents.

After a few minutes of craziness, my brother and I ran out to the driveway basketball goal to pretend that we were the Hoosiers playing in the Final Four. When the phone rang, I ran inside and began talking to my mom, who was standing at the door of "The Pit." We began talking about the game and how excited we were, and she would periodically say, "Oh, here comes Greg Graham and Damon Bailey," which was followed by cheers from other fans.

Then she said that someone else there wanted to talk to me. So, thinking that it was my father, I said, "We did it, Dad!" The response was unexpected. "Chad, this isn't your dad, it's Calbert." I still thought it was my dad playing a joke on me, so I said, "Whatever, Dad." The reply from the other end was, "No, this is really Calbert Cheaney." As soon as it hit me that I was talking to my favorite IU player ever, my jaw dropped to the floor and I was so excited that I don't really remember much of what was said for the rest of the conversation. It was a wonderful moment of my life that will always bring a huge smile to my face."

—Chad Tolliver
Student, 1995 – 1999

IU IQ

The two members of the '82-83 team who were five-year roommates were:
 a. Jim Thomas and Ted Kitchel
 b. Ted Kitchel and Randy Wittman
 c. Randy Wittman and Tony Brown
 d. Tony Brown and Steve Bouchie

Who was the only Knight player who played the entire game, forty minutes, 45 times?
 a. Quinn Buckner
 b. Randy Wittman
 c. Steve Alford
 d. Damon Bailey

Two IU basketball players were in the 1984 Olympics but on different teams. Who were they?

In 1985, which Hoosier completed the Big Ten season and still holds the conference record with a free-throw percentage of .935?
 a. Marty Simmons
 b. Delray Brooks
 c. Winston Morgan
 d. Steve Alford

Which Hoosier broke his right wrist in the NCAA final game against Syracuse?
 a. Steve Alford
 b. Rick Calloway
 c. Joe Hillman
 d. Daryl Thomas

Complete this well known phrase regarding Steve Alford's free-throw shooting. "Socks, shorts, 1, 2, 3, _____."

This '87-88 player had 90 more blocks than his closest teammate:

March 13, 1983

Victory over OSU gives Big
Ten title to Indiana at
Assembly Hall; five players
speak at Senior Day

December 7, 1985

Steve Alford is given a one-game
suspension for appearing in a
charity calendar. Alford misses the
Kentucky game in Lexington and IU
loses, 58-63

February 23, 1985

Bob Knight hurls
chair across court
during Purdue game
and is ejected

January 15, 1987

Steve Alford scores
2000th collegiate point
on a 3 pointer at
Assembly Hall against
Wisconsin

IU IQ

Magnus Pelkowski was from what city and country?
- a. London, England
- b. Munich, Germany
- c. Warsaw, Poland
- d. Bogata, Columbia

The '88-89 team holds the Indiana record for:
- a. Free- throw attempts
- b. Three-point percentage
- c. points
- d. field-goal attempts

The only IU freshman to score 20 points as a starter in the season opener was:
- a. Quinn Buckner
- b. A. J. Guyton
- c. Steve Alford
- d. Calbert Cheaney

The first left-handed starter for Bob Knight was:
- a. Lyndon Jones
- b. Jim Crews
- c. Pat Graham
- d. Calbert Cheaney

The leading rebounder on the '91-92 team was:
- a. Calbert Cheaney
- b. Alan Henderson
- c. Eric Anderson
- d. Greg Graham

Which nonconference team did IU play twice during the 1991-1992 season?
- a. UCLA
- b. Kentucky
- c. Butler
- d. Notre Dame

Answers: b. Ted Kitchel and Randy Wittman; b. Randy Wittman; Steve Alford (USA) and Uwe Blab (West Germany); d. Steve Alford; b. Rick Calloway; Swoosh; Dean Garrett; d. Bogata, Columbia; a. Free- throw attempts; d. Calbert Cheaney; d. Calbert Cheaney; b. Alan Henderson; a. UCLA

March 30, 1987	January 9, 1989	April, 1991	March 28, 1992
Indiana claims fifth National Championship when "The Shot" brings victory over Syracuse in final game, 74-73	Bob Knight becomes the Big Ten's winningest coach	Coach Bob Knight receives the honor of National Basketball Hall of Fame induction	The Pit is the scene of Indiana's victory over UCLA, 106-79

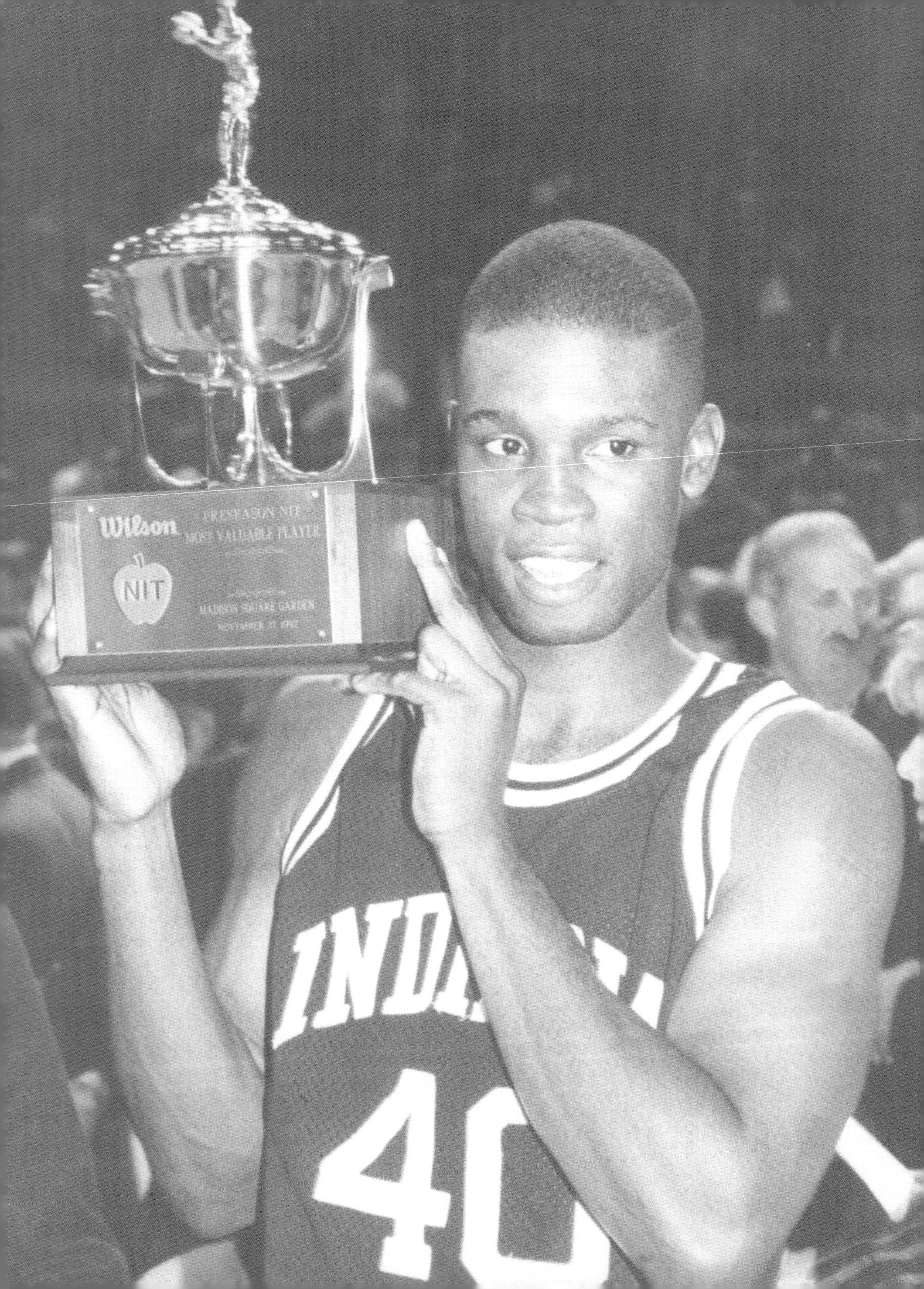
Wilson
PRESEASON NIT
MOST VALUABLE PLAYER
NIT
MADISON SQUARE GARDEN
40

19

1992 – 1993

A Sterling Era Comes to an End

FEW groups have accomplished more. When Calbert Cheaney, Matt Nover, Greg Graham and Chris Reynolds departed the streets of Bloomington, they left a standard of play followers will strive for but few will achieve. In four years, the Hoosiers posted a 105-27 record. They claimed two Big Ten crowns, made it to the Sweet Sixteen three times and the Final Four once.

1992-1993 saw the Hoosiers flying high and ranked no lower than sixth in the nation the entire season. For five weeks they held the No. 2 slot. For five weeks they were No. 1. With both inside and outside weapons, it was a season of Hoosier dominance.

The roll began when IU earned the Preseason NIT title by winning two games at Assembly Hall and traveling to New York City to claim the trophy. After defeating Florida State in overtime, the Hoosiers downed Seton Hall in the final game. Unfortunately, Pat Graham, who sat out the previous year, rebroke his left foot during the FSU fray. Premier player Calbert Cheaney grabbed national attention with a great tournament performance and was named Most Valuable Player. Cheaney gave Graham the MVP trophy on the plane ride back to Indiana.

From November through most of February, the Hoosiers notched 23 wins against two losses, falling only to No. 3 Kansas and No. 3 Kentucky. The stretch included eleven games won by twenty or more points and two victories over Michigan's acclaimed Fab Five. Although Cheaney was the primary scorer, offensive support came from all members of the team. Alan Henderson logged several double doubles in the record book as he became a huge inside threat and played a major role in IU's success. Then came the injury.

In practice two days before the Purdue game, Henderson tore the anterior cruciate ligament in his right knee, and the Hoosier faithful held their breath. Where do we go from here?

Team Roster 1992-1993
(Overall 31-4, Big Ten 17-1)

#	Player	Pos.	Year
11	Malcolm Sims	G	F
20	Greg Graham	G	S
21	Chris Reynolds	G	S
22	Damon Bailey	G	J
24	Matt Nover	C	S
25	Pat Knight	G	So
30	Todd Leary	G	J
33	Pat Graham	G	J
34	Brian Evans	F	F
40	Calbert Cheaney	F	S
44	Alan Henderson	F	So
50	Todd Lindeman	C	So

ABOVE LEFT
Chris Reynolds used quickness to become a great defensive player.

124

Bob Knight responded with a retooled lineup of three guards that included Damon Bailey. With Greg Graham hitting a record 26 of 28 free throws and scoring 32, Indiana defeated Purdue in Assembly Hall. Pat Graham returned to the lineup, and Brian Evans contributed with 20 points. The next game Indiana came up short, however, and lost by three at Ohio State. The possibility of an undefeated Big Ten season was gone.

A milestone in Indiana history took place on March 4, 1993 when Calbert Cheaney hit a three-pointer to break the all-time scoring record at Indiana and in the Big Ten. During a time-out, the senior forward was presented the game ball at halfcourt while fans roared with appreciation.

A first-place finish in conference play netted another Big Ten title.

The NCAA rewarded IU with the No. 1 seed in the Midwest Regional, and the Hoosiers played first-round games in their backyard, the Indianapolis Hoosier Dome. Showing how much they love Indiana basketball, 25,000 people showed up at the Dome to watch the Hoosiers practice. To show their appreciation, Bob Knight, assistant coaches and players laid on the floor to form the letters *THANKS*.

A 43-point win over Wright State was followed by a challenging and narrow defeat of Xavier. IU made it to the Elite Eight by downing Louisville, but could not overcome a strong Kansas team.

Disappointed, yes. But the sterling record speaks for itself.

A Player Remembers

We had really high expectations, and we really lived up to them throughout the course of the year and through all the regular season We were rolling. I mean, we were No. 1 for a long time. We won a lot of games in a row and beat a lot of quality teams on their court or at our place.

It was definitely the best team out of the four years we had. No, it was just unfortunate that I couldn't help out like I wanted to after I tore my ACL in February. It threw a slight kink in our plans. But we still made a good run and a good push at it and got all the way to the final eight, but we just couldn't get it done."

—Alan Henderson
Forward/Center, 1992 – 1995
All-American, 1995

20

1993 – 1994,
1994 – 1995,
1995 – 1996

Great Players, Respectable Years

THE next three seasons of IU basketball shared a similar theme. Each year featured a prominent, nationally recognized player who spent his last year playing on a moderately excellent, though not top-tiered, team.

Few players have ever received the attention Damon Bailey experienced. Since his eighth grade year, the basketball world had taken note of the kid from Heltonville. With such notoriety came hopes and expectations. Throughout his four-year career at Indiana, Damon handled that pressure by giving ultimate effort and playing team basketball.

LEFT
Alan Henderson is the rebounding king of Indiana. During four years he recorded 1,091 boards.

When the '93-94 season got off to a rocky start with a surprising loss at Butler's Hinkle Fieldhouse, the next game against No. 1 ranked Kentucky looked like a pretty daunting task. To the surprise of 39,197 fans in the Hoosier Dome, Indiana responded with sharp, enthused play and at game's end led the Wildcats 96-84.

The season was sprinkled with ups and downs and injuries. Finishing third in the Big Ten at 12-6, the Hoosiers advanced to the Regional Semifinal game of the NCAA Tournament before losing to Boston College. Seniors Pat Graham, Todd Leary, and Damon Bailey finished their last year at IU with a respectable 21-9 record. Bailey was named to the All-Big Ten team and third team All-American.

'94 -95—The last two years of standout Alan Henderson's IU career were statistically awesome. He departed Indiana as the record setter for rebounds, blocks and double doubles. The power forward scored 20 or more points in 24 of 31 games in the '94-95 season. His rebounds totaled 1,091 in four years.

A new group of five freshmen joined the roster in the fall and blended with the team to accrue a decent 19 and 12 record. A consistent offense was lacking for the '94-95 Hoosiers, but an outstanding defense that held opponents to a field shooting percentage of only .410 was their strength.

Senior Day at Assembly Hall was special this year. Coach Knight spoke highly of seniors Todd Leary and Alan Henderson and then emotionally turned his attention to his favorite Indiana player ever, son Pat Knight.

LEFT
Damon's career brought selection for Indiana's MVP, Big Ten Freshman of the Year, First Team All-Big Ten, and Third Team All-American. His emotional farewell speech on Senior Day on March 12, 1994 is remembered by many.

RIGHT
From Channing, Michigan, Todd Lindeman was the second 7-foot Hoosier.

The '95-96 version of the Hoosiers averaged 75.8 points per game and proved to be one of the best offensive teams of the Big Ten. They were also a good defensive unit, holding opposing teams to a .409 shooting percentage.

Brian Evans was the senior star and the first Knight player to lead the Big Ten in scoring. Evans's offensive stats were impressive, and he led the conference in many offensive categories. He scored 658 points in his senior season and was also the team leader in rebounds with 221. The Big Ten Conference awarded the forward the Most Valuable Player trophy.

A Fan Remembers

"**B**rian Evans dislocated his shoulder during the Big Ten season in '94 but continued to play. During an important game his shoulder again moved out of place. Obviously in pain, but unwilling to leave the game, Brian walked to the corner of the floor and as much as possible turned his back to the crowd. He then popped his shoulder back into place and returned to the game. Ouch! What a warrior."

LEFT
Bob Knight's first player to win the Big Ten season scoring title was Brian Evans in 1996.

Team Roster 1994-1995 (Overall 19-12, Big Ten 11-7, Tied for Third in Conference)

#	Player	Pos.	Year
3	Charlie Miller	G/F	F
5	Neil Reed	G	F
20	Sherron Wilkerson	G	So
21	Richard Mandeville	C	So
23	Steve Hart	G	So
25	Pat Knight	G	S
30	Michael Hermon	G	F
32	Robbie Eggers	F	F
33	Rob Hodgson	F	F
34	Brian Evans	F	J
44	Alan Henderson	F	S
45	Andrae Patterson	F	F
50	Todd Lindeman	C	J

Team Roster 1993-1994 (Overall 21-9, Big Ten 12 – 6, Third in Conference)

#	Player	Pos.	Year
12	Robert Foster	G	F
20	Sherron Wilkerson	G	F
21	Richard Mandeville	C	F
22	Damon Bailey	G	S
23	Steve Hart	G	F
25	Pat Knight	G	J
30	Todd Leary	G	S
32	Robbie Eggers	F	F
33	Pat Graham	G	S
34	Brian Evans	F	So
44	Alan Henderson	F	J
50	Todd Lindeman	C	So

Team Roster 1995-1996 (Overall 19-12, Big Ten 12-6, Tied for Second in Conference)

#	Player	Pos.	Year
3	Charlie Miller	G	So
4	Chris Rowles	G	So
5	Neil Reed	G	So
20	Sherron Wilkerson	G	So
21	Richard Mandeville	C	So
32	Robbie Eggers	F	So
33	Larry Richardson	F	F
34	Brian Evans	F	S
42	Lou Moore	G/F	So
45	Andrae Patterson	F	So
50	Todd Lindeman	C	S
55	Harris Mujezinovic	C	J

21

1996 – 1997, 1997 – 1998, 1998 – 1999, 1999 – 2000

Middle of the Road

TWENTY wins per season are considered a benchmark of a success. Using that standard, the Indiana basketball program of the late nineties was certainly successful. The next four years of Hoosier hoops were full of accomplishments and shining moments. And yet, when each season came to a close, few were content with the campaign.

Out of the starting blocks, the preconference records were always promising: 14-1, 9-3, 13-2 and 10-1. Then January and the realities of Big Ten play repeatedly brought IU teams back down to earth. Conference standings of sixth place, fifth place, third place, and another fifth reflect a streak of mediocrity unfamiliar to the Indiana basketball community. NCAA Tournament play that consisted of one or two games and out left an unsettling feeling as Hoosier teams battled but were unable to advance.

LEFT
The Florida 5A Player of the Year achieved Honorable Mention All-Big Ten.

'96-97—Winning the Chase Preseason NIT initiated another fine group of freshmen into the winning ways of Indiana basketball. Andrae Patterson blasted Duke in the final game of the tournament with 39 points and was awarded the NIT Most Valuable Player. Led by A. J. Guyton, who as a freshman claimed team scoring honors, the team posted a 22-11 record that featured close games and many moments of freshman play.

Accolades were given to Coach Bob Knight as he won his 700th career game and became the youngest Big Ten Coach to accomplish such a feat.

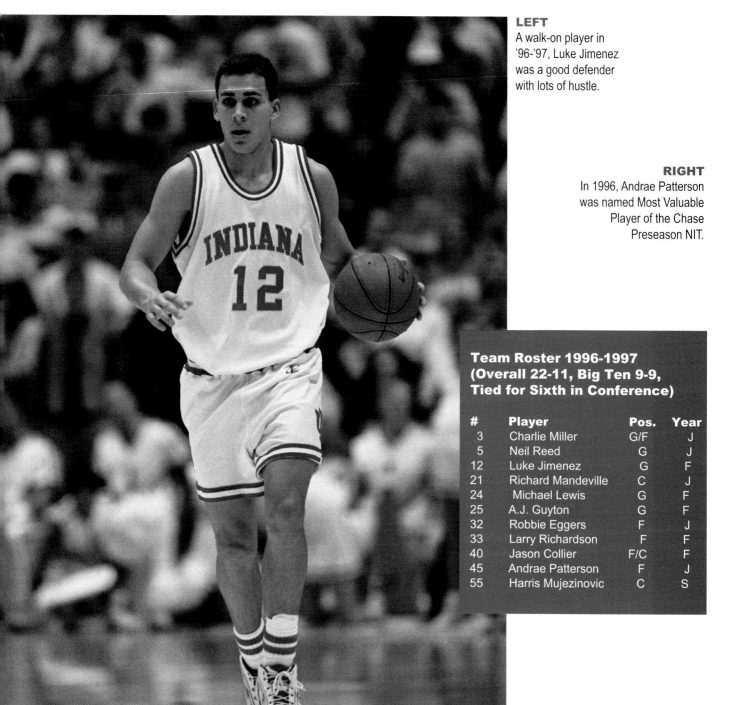

LEFT
A walk-on player in '96-'97, Luke Jimenez was a good defender with lots of hustle.

RIGHT
In 1996, Andrae Patterson was named Most Valuable Player of the Chase Preseason NIT.

Team Roster 1996-1997 (Overall 22-11, Big Ten 9-9, Tied for Sixth in Conference)

#	Player	Pos.	Year
3	Charlie Miller	G/F	J
5	Neil Reed	G	J
12	Luke Jimenez	G	F
21	Richard Mandeville	C	J
24	Michael Lewis	G	F
25	A.J. Guyton	G	F
32	Robbie Eggers	F	J
33	Larry Richardson	F	F
40	Jason Collier	F/C	F
45	Andrae Patterson	F	J
55	Harris Mujezinovic	C	S

Team Roster 1997-1998
(Overall 20-12, Big Ten 9-7,
Tied for Fifth in Conference)

#	Player	Pos.	Year
3	Charlie Miller	F	S
4	Luke Recker	G/F	F
12	Luke Jimenez	G	So
21	Richard Mandeville	C	S
23	Rob Turner	G	J
24	Michael Lewis	G	So
25	A.J. Guyton	G	So
30	William Gladness	F	J
32	Robbie Eggers	F	S
35	Kirk Haston	F/C	F
40	Jason Collier	C	So
45	Andrae Patterson	F	S
53	Tom Geyer	F	F

'97-98—Shouts of "Luuuke" resonated in Assembly Hall for the first time as the long-awaited Indiana Mr. Basketball joined the Hoosier troops. Recker joined a strong scoring and shooting team and scored in double figures nineteen times as a freshman. Senior Andrae Patterson excelled at the end of the season, and sophomore Michael Lewis emerged as the team's leader in assists. A. J. Guyton followed his fabulous freshman debut with a sensational sophomore year and was named to the Media All-Conference first team. The Hoosiers continued the tradition of claiming both the Indiana Classic and Hoosier Classic titles and closed 20-12 for 1997-1998.

LEFT
Michael Lewis dished out 545 assists during his college career and is IU's all-time assist leader.

**Team Roster 1998-1999
(Overall 23-11, Big Ten 9-7,
Tied for Third in Conference)**

#	Player	Pos.	Year
4	Luke Recker	G/F	So
10	Antwaan Randle El	G	F
11	Dane Fife	G	F
12	Luke Jimenez	G	J
23	Rob Turner	G	S
24	Michael Lewis	G	J
25	A.J. Guyton	G	J
30	William Gladness	F	S
32	Kyle Hornsby	G/F	F
33	Larry Richardson	F	J
35	Kirk Haston	F/C	F
43	Jarrad Odle	F	F
44	Lynn Washington	F	J
53	Tom Geyer	F	F

The 1998-1999 season thrilled fans with a record-setting seven overtime games including one double overtime tussle at Penn State. Indiana prevailed in OT on four of those occasions. In a year when IU was the top scoring team in the Big Ten, newcomer Kirk Haston drew attention with twenty games in double figures. Teammate A. J. Guyton made 67 three-point shots for the year and became Indiana's all-time leader in trey attempts.

Luke Recker, the leading scorer on the team, shocked the Hoosier world with his postseason announcement that his career at Indiana had ended. He departed to play at Arizona.

RIGHT
A crowd favorite, Luke Recker led the Hoosiers in points and steals his sophomore year.

Team Roster 1999-2000
(Overall 20-9, Big Ten 10-6,
Fifth in Conference)

#	Player	Pos.	Year
3	Tom Coverdale	G	F
5	George Leach	C/F	F
10	Antwaan Randle El	G	So
11	Dane Fife	G	So
12	Luke Jimenez	G	S
24	Michael Lewis	G	S
25	A.J. Guyton	G	S
32	Kyle Hornsby	G/F	F
33	Larry Richardson	F	S
35	Kirk Haston	F/C	So
43	Jarrad Odle	F	So
44	Lynn Washington	F	S
50	Jeffrey Newton	F	F
53	Tom Geyer	F	F

The pattern of the three preceding years continued into 1999-2000. Ten nonconference wins were dotted with only one surprising loss to Indiana State in the Indiana Classic. The end of December found Hoosier fans hopeful for a Big Ten breakout year. When conference play ended, the IU record stood at 10-6 with another fifth-place finish.

Standout A. J. Guyton was the leading scorer in 18 of the season's 29 games. Guyton was honored by a first team All-Big Ten selection and named Big Ten Player of the Year. Senior Michael Lewis finished at the top of Indiana's list of career assists by dishing out 545 assists.

A Player Remembers

"The best thing that happened for my wife and I as a family was because of the Illinois game at Indiana in 1998. It was February 24th and was the night that Coach Knight and Ted Valentine had their altercations throughout the game. Valentine threw Coach Knight out. We were fortunate in that the school and the coaching staff allowed former players to come back and sit right behind the bench, which is probably a little bit too close for me. I can remember running up and down the sidelines chasing Valentine out of the hallway at halftime. My wife was pregnant with our first kid. She is almost as bad a fan as I am and was screaming and yelling about the situation. With ten minutes to go in that game, her water broke. All that screaming and yelling probably had a little something to do with it. We left the game, called the doctor, drove back to Indianapolis and about 1:30 the next day, our first son, Max, was born."

—Todd Leary
Guard, 1989 – 1994
Indiana University Basketball Broadcaster

RIGHT
A. J. Guyton: All-American,
Big Ten MVP, Indiana Most
Valuable Player four years—
An Indiana Great!

The end of the 2000 season brought controversy with long-reaching effects. Days before the NCAA Tournament began, ESPN broke a story of Neil Reed's ('95-97) claim, supported by video footage, that Coach Knight had choked him during a practice. It was the beginning of the end of a very long chapter in Indiana basketball history.

With a wildfire of negative debate surrounding Coach Knight, the players and the university, IU lost the first game of the tournament to Pepperdine. It was Bob Knight's last game as head coach of Indiana University men's basketball.

22

2000

The Painful Departure of Coach Bob Knight

On a Sunday afternoon, September 10, 2000, president Myles Brand announced the termination of Bob Knight as head coach of Indiana University basketball. The announcement marked the end of an era: twenty-nine seasons of championships, hard-nosed competition, high graduation rates, honors, pride. Moments of controversy at regular intervals were part of the era as well.

The breakup was not amicable and involved students, players, coaches, administrators, attorneys, alumni, fans, and citizens of the state of Indiana. The national spotlight focused on Bloomington as the uncomfortable adjustment took place.

Bob Knight has been referred to as "The Most Influential Coach in America." His record at Indiana speaks for itself:

- Overall Indiana Record: 661-240 (.734)
- Big Ten Record : 353-151 (.700)
- Three NCAA Championships ('76, '81, '87)
- Eleven Big Ten Championships
- One National Invitational Tournament Championship ('79)
- Four-time National Coach of the Year ('75, '76, '87, '89)
- Coach of nine Big Ten MVPs
- Coach of gold medal U.S. Pan-American team ('79)
- Coach of gold medal USA Olympic Team ('84)

LEFT
Bob Knight arrived at Indiana in 1971 and brought twenty-nine years of basketball excellence.

141

A new coach takes the
reins of the men's
basketball program.

23
2000 – 2001

New Coach, New Beginnings and Success Under Clouds

TO follow the footsteps of a legend is a difficult thing. Mike Davis was given the task when athletic director Clarence Doninger named Davis interim head coach on September 12, 2000. In the midst of a storm, the Indiana assistant coach from Fayette, Alabama inherited a team with no seniors only eight weeks before the season was to tip off.

The forty-year-old arrived in Bloomington in 1997 after serving as an assistant coach at his alma mater, the University of Alabama. As a player for the Crimson Tide, Davis earned the team Hustle Award each of his four seasons and his senior year was named to the SEC's All-Defensive team. Following college, Davis played professional ball in Europe and the CBA. While with the Witchita Falls Texans, he was both an assistant and player under John Treloar, now IU's associate head coach.

Focusing on the task at hand, the Hoosiers entered the new season resolved to carry on the successful tradition of Indiana basketball. Hoosier fans watched with trepidation.

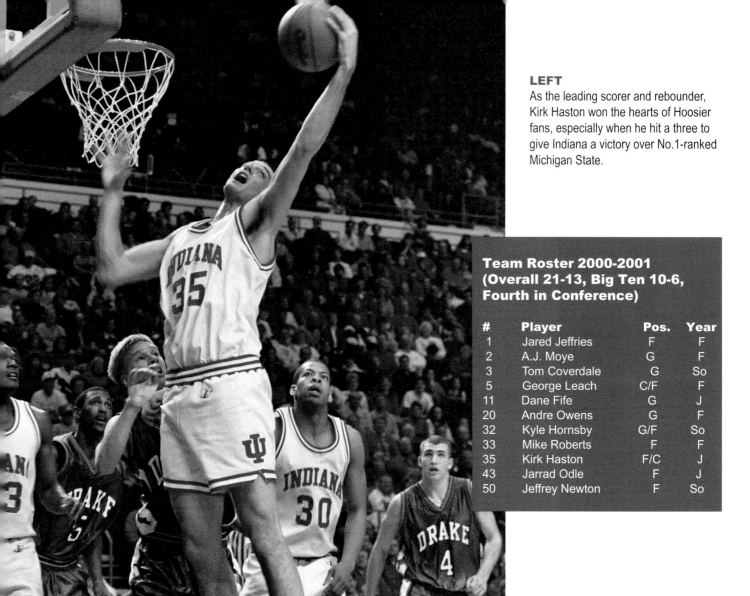

**Team Roster 2000-2001
(Overall 21-13, Big Ten 10-6,
Fourth in Conference)**

#	Player	Pos.	Year
1	Jared Jeffries	F	F
2	A.J. Moye	G	F
3	Tom Coverdale	G	So
5	George Leach	C/F	F
11	Dane Fife	G	J
20	Andre Owens	G	F
32	Kyle Hornsby	G/F	So
33	Mike Roberts	F	F
35	Kirk Haston	F/C	J
43	Jarrad Odle	F	J
50	Jeffrey Newton	F	So

IU opened play in the Preseason NIT by defeating both Pepperdine and South Alabama before dropping the next two tournament games. Early on, one of the obvious changes from the previous year was the dramatically increased role for sophomore guard Tom Coverdale, whose playing time jumped from only 41 minutes in 2000 to 1160 minutes in 2001.

Perhaps the low point of the season came in the December loss to Kentucky in Louisville. In the postgame conference, both players and coach were visibly discouraged. Two weeks later, the Hoosiers bounced back for the biggest win of the year. In front of a home crowd on January 7, 2001, on the last shot of the game, center Kirk Haston hit a three-pointer to put IU ahead 59-58 over No. 1-ranked Michigan State. It was an Assembly Hall first, the only time Indiana had beaten a No. 1-ranked team on McCracken Memorial Court.

Conference play ended with a fourth-place standing at 10-6. The Big Ten Tournament, however, brought a new experience for IU. After beating Wisconsin, 64-52, in game one, the Hoosiers knocked off the tournament's No. 1 seed, Illinois, 58-56 and for the first time ever advanced to the championship game. With Indiana's own Steve Alford at the helm of Iowa, IU fell to the Hawkeyes in the last few seconds, 63-61. The season then closed with a first-game NCAA loss to Kent State.

In his first year as coach, Mike Davis and team established a 21-13 record and brought Hoosier fans some thrills in the process. Twenty-one wins are the most victories for a first-year coach in Indiana's basketball history. Kirk Haston was named first team All-Big Ten and Jared Jeffries Big Ten Freshman of the Year.

The baton was passed. The exchange was not the smoothest, but the racers survived and continued on to reach the finish line in good standing. The Indiana University basketball legacy lives on.

A Coach Reflects

"It was scary, to be honest with you, because of the tradition of Indiana. When I was the one named interim coach, walking out on the court for the first time knowing that I was in charge of a great program was intimidating at first. It's definitely a privilege and an honor, and it just gives you an unbelievable feeling to be a part of that, especially when you're playing at home and the fans are cheering at the beginning of the game."

—Mike Davis, when asked about his thoughts when named interim coach
Indiana Head Coach, 2000 – Present
Assistant Coach, 1997 – 2000

A Player Reflects

"In that year, he [Mike Davis] got that chance and he did well. The university and the state of Indiana is very fortunate to get Coach Davis."

—Dane Fife, when asked about his thoughts and his decision to stay at IU in 2000
Guard, 1998 – 2002

24
2001 – 2002

We're Baaaaaack!!!

WHEN junior Kirk Haston announced that he was leaving IU to enter the NBA draft in the spring, the look of the upcoming team changed drastically. The departure of Haston meant the loss of the team's top scorer in 21 games and leading rebounder of 20 games. Big shoes to fill!

By the time November rolled around, adjustments were made and the prospect of a Big Ten title drove the Hoosiers as the season began. An unusual schedule had Indiana play the first six games of the season away and included trips to Charlotte, North Carolina, Anchorage, Alaska, a return to the Tar Heel state with a final destination of Carbondale, Illinois before playing in the friendly confines of Assembly Hall. The result of the early road trip was a 4-2 record and over 8,500 miles of travel.

RIGHT
The 2002 Big Ten Player of the Year, Jared Jeffries, led Indiana in points and rebounds.

LEFT
The Mideast Regional's MVP climbs the ladder, ice pack and all, to claim his share of the nets.

OPPOSITE BOTTOM RIGHT
Jarrad Odle's excellent season and all-around play helped Indiana advance to Atlanta.

The first game of the season in Assembly Hall was on December 4th as the road-weary Hoosiers squeaked by a good Notre Dame team, 76-75. Another intrastate battle followed against Ball State, who was ranked No. 15. IU prevailed by thirteen. Conseco Fieldhouse in Indianapolis was the scene of Indiana's first-ever loss in the Hoosier Classic as Butler claimed the Classic crown by two points.

In the opening moments of the Big Ten clash at Northwestern, starter George Leach suffered an ankle injury, and Jarrad Odle came off the bench to score sixteen points and collect fifteen rebounds in the IU victory. It was the beginning of great things for Odle, who was the leading rebounder in seven games before the season ended. Wins over Michigan State and Iowa left fans daring to hope that maybe, just maybe, this could be a season of serious contention. It had been so long!

On January 26th, the eighth-ranked Illini came calling at Assembly Hall. Before they knew what hit them, Indiana hit a record 17 three-point shots and convincingly controlled the game, 88-57. Dane Fife, who was known as a defensive specialist, knocked down six threes and scored a total of 20 points. Assembly Hall was loud and rocking and alive again.

Losses sprinkled throughout Big Ten play kept the season interesting. When IU claimed a portion of the Big Ten crown with a victory over Northwestern in the final conference game, the

Hoosier faithful were overjoyed. 1993 was the last time the Big Ten trophy had found a home in Bloomington.

The team entered the Big Ten Tournament confident and excited. A win over MSU set up a semifinal game against Iowa which featured former IU star Luke Recker as their "go to" man. Recker came through and with only seconds remaining hit a shot to give Iowa the win.

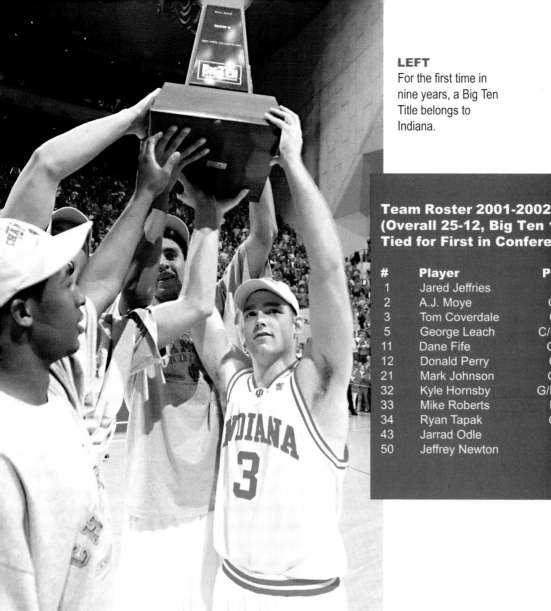

Team Roster 2001-2002 (Overall 25-12, Big Ten 11-5, Tied for First in Conference)

#	Player	Pos.	Year
1	Jared Jeffries	F	So
2	A.J. Moye	G	So
3	Tom Coverdale	G	J
5	George Leach	C/F	So
11	Dane Fife	G	S
12	Donald Perry	G	F
21	Mark Johnson	G	F
32	Kyle Hornsby	G/F	J
33	Mike Roberts	F	So
34	Ryan Tapak	G	F
43	Jarrad Odle	F	S
50	Jeffrey Newton	F	J

Seeded No. 5 in the South Regionals, the team trekked to Sacramento for their first match with Rick Majerus's Utah. In the last seven years of NCAA competition, first-round games meant elimination for Indiana on five occasions and second-round games two times. Would the pattern continue? A 19-point victory over the Utes followed by a 76-67 defeat of UNC Wilmington (who had upset USC in the first game) advanced the Hoosiers to the Sweet Sixteen.

The next task was formidable, as No. 1-ranked Duke awaited Indiana in Lexington. No one gave IU a chance. The defending national champions controlled the first half and at one point commanded a 17-point lead. The Hoosiers continued to scrape and hustle and worked themselves back into the game. Assistant coach Jim Thomas recalls the point when he felt his team was going to win:

"When Coverdale came back in the game, we made our run. A. J. Moye blocked a shot by Boozer, and then I think Coverdale came down and he made a turnaround jumper to put us up by one point. I could see the confidence in our body language, and I saw the way the Duke guys looked, that they were a little petrified. It was a little bit more than they could handle. They are used to getting out on people and people kind of wilting, and they make a little run, but the score is so big that they can't do anything. So when they realized that wasn't going to happen, you could see on their faces that, you know, we've got a ballgame here. We are in a lot of trouble. That was kind of a nice feeling to have, because so many people had counted us out. But I think a lot of faithful felt that anything could happen."

With one minute remaining, Coverdale hit his only field goal of the game to give IU its first lead. A. J. Moye stood at the foul line with eleven seconds remaining and a 72-70 lead. Senior Dane Fife reflects, "I recall it was ours with Moye at the free-throw line when he had two shots to put us up four. And I said, 'A. J., you make these two and we're going to the Final Four. We're going all the way, Baby!' And he put them in, and the rest of the story … it doesn't end that simple [laugh] … the rest of the story."

What Fife was referring to were the final agonizing seconds of the game. With Indiana leading 74-70 and 4.2 seconds remaining, Jason Williams shot and hit a three-pointer and was fouled by Fife. The score was 74-73 with Williams at the stripe. A miss by Williams was rebounded by teammate Carlos Boozer with .04 on the clock. His put-back attempt failed, and Hoosier Jeff Newton grabbed the rebound and the game.

Pandemonium erupted at Rupp Arena. The unbelievably large sea of Hoosier red that filled the seats wildly celebrated the shocking victory. The disappointment and frustration of recent years were released in the joyous, euphoric moments following the upset.

The Regional Final against Kent State was played against another backdrop of red. It was as if Assembly Hall had been relocated to Lexington, Kentucky. Indiana bombarded Kent by hitting 15 of 19 treys and controlled most of the game. Guard Tom Coverdale went down late in the game with an ankle injury, and for a few moments the game tightened, but the 81-69 final score meant that Indiana would travel to the Final Four.

RIGHT
The smile says it all!
Dane Fife and the
Hoosiers are going to the
Final Four.

IU was joined by Oklahoma, Kansas and Maryland in Atlanta. Once again, the Hoosiers were considered an "also ran" and given little chance of playing in the final game. Once again, the team and fans found delight in proving the experts wrong. A tough defense held the Oklahoma offense to 36.4 shooting percentage. Jeff Newton and A. J. Moye sparked the team in front of their hometown crowd.

Indiana had not appeared in a championship game since 1987. A victory was not to be, and the Hoosier heroes fell to the Maryland Terrapins, 52-64.

The March NCAA Tournament run will be etched in the memories of Hoosier fans forever. It

ABOVE
Jeff Newton's outstanding tournament play helped take him home to the Georgia Dome.

was special! Indiana broadcaster Don Fischer reflects, "It was the most fun that I think a team could have. And the fun they were having translated into fun and excitement for the fans. The entire experience, from the first-round win over Utah, to the stunning upset of Duke, then the trip to the Final Four and another shocker over Oklahoma, all served to create a healing environment for a program that had gone through two years of chaos. The poison atmosphere is now gone, and the great tradition of IU basketball can again flourish as it has through most of its storied history."

Indiana players and fans lived a joyous dream in 2002.

A Player Remembers

"I think that Coach Davis would recognize the fact that the bus was too tense or that we were all too tense, so he'd send [his young son] Antoine to the back of the bus. We'd mess around with Antoine and joke with him and pretty much tortured him back there. But it gave everybody a laugh and released the tension that we had."

—Dane Fife, when asked to share a favorite inside moment
Guard, 1998 – 2002

RIGHT
Antoine does his part to help the team.

LEFT
Junior Kyle Hornsby helped bombard opponents with threes.

A Player Reflects

"I just enjoyed especially the Final Four and really the Duke game, when they beat Duke. That was a highlight. That's a recent memory, obviously.

And then going down to the Final Four in Atlanta this year and seeing them beat Oklahoma in that game and getting in the final game. That was so unexpected. I just was happy for the coach and the players and all the coaches. They'd been through an awful lot and I think it was a neat process or a healing time for the whole university. It seems like it brought a lot of people back together that maybe had been fragmented and discouraged over the past several years."

—Tom Abernethy, when asked about anything that stands out about IU basketball since he played
Forward, 1972 – 1976
Final Four All Tournament Team, 1976

A Coach Comments

"That was awesome. It was unbelievable. I think it gave all Indiana fans pride and happiness when that shot went in. No matter what the outcome would have been, just going up two points late in the game like that gave the belief that they could build it back. That's a game that everybody thinks about when they think about our season this year. It's not losing to Maryland. It's not beating Oklahoma. It's beating Duke."

—Mike Davis, referring to Coverdale's go-ahead shot in the Duke regional game
Indiana Head Coach, 2000 – Present
Assistant Coach, 1997 – 2000

RIGHT
Coach Mike Davis takes a moment to enjoy the spotlight.

IU IQ

The '92-93 team boasts the highest-scoring duo for a season in IU history. Who was the duo?
a. Calbert Cheaney and Greg Graham
b. Calbert Cheaney and Alan Henderson
c. Calbert Cheaney and Matt Nover
d. Calbert Cheaney and Damon Bailey

During the '92-93 season, Ivan Renko played this role in Indiana basketball:
a. was a junior college transfer who stayed at IU for only one semester
b. became a beloved student manager for the Hoosiers
c. spent his first year at IU as an assistant coach
d. was an imaginary recruit from Yugoslavia Coach Knight mentioned to the press

The Hollywood star who spent time in Bloomington with Bob Knight as he prepared to play a coach in the movie *Blue Chips* was:
a. Denzel Washington
b. Brian Dennehy
c. Tom Cruise
d. Nick Nolte

Which senior on the '93-94 team did Knight speak of when saying, 'He had a heart bigger than his body .·' I bought him for nothing and wouldn't sell him for gold.'
a. Damon Bailey
b. Todd Leary
c. Pat Graham
d. Alan Henderson

The player who holds the IU record for playing in the most NCAA Tournament victories (11) is:
a. Quinn Buchner
b. Steve Alford
c. Calbert Cheaney
d. Damon Bailey

Who were the five Mr. Basketballs on the 2001-2002 team?

December 4, 1993	January 6, 1993	December 4, 1993	March 20, 1994
Indiana defeats No. 1-ranked Kentucky at Hoosier Dome	Home victory over Iowa makes Bob Knight the youngest NCAA coach to win 600 games	Indiana defeats No. 1-ranked Kentucky at Hoosier Dome	In NCAA Regional game, IU wins but loses Sherron Wilkerson, who broke his leg in the second half

IU IQ

The only Hoosier in Assembly Hall history to have two seasons of 300-plus rebounds is:
   a. Steve Downing
   b. Kent Benson
   c. Alan Henderson
   d. Andrae Patterson

The number of Big Ten Conference games was reduced to ___ in 1998 because of the Big Ten Tournament.
   a. 18
   b. 17
   c. 16
   d. 14

This '98-99 Hoosier was named an Academic All-American.
   a. Luke Jimenez
   b. Luke Recker
   c. A. J. Guyton
   d. Michael Lewis

Which 2000-2001 player was the Mr. Basketball of Georgia?
   a. Dane Fife
   b. Kirk Haston
   c. Andre Owens
   d. A.J. Moye

The assist leader on the 2000-2001 team was:
   a. Dane Fife
   b. Tom Coverdale
   c. A. J. Moye
   d. Kyle Hornsby

In 2002 IU shared the Big Ten title with what other schools?

Answers: a. Calbert Cheaney and Greg Graham (785 pts and 577 pts); d. was an imaginary recruit from Yugoslavia Coach Knight mentioned to the press; d. Nick Nolte
b. Todd Leary; d. Damon Bailey; Jared Jeffries, Indiana; A. J. Moye, Georgia; Tom Coverdale, Indiana; Dane Fife, Michigan; Donald Perry, Louisiana;
c. Alan Henderson ('94: 308,'95: 302); c.16; b. Luke Recker; d. A. J. Moye; b. Tom Coverdale; Wisconsin, Ohio State and Illinois

September 10, 2000	September 12, 2000	January 27, 2002	April 2, 2002
Bob Knight is terminated as head coach of Indiana University	Assistant coach Mike Davis becomes interim head coach of Indiana	Indiana hits a record 17 three point shots and downs eighth-ranked Illinois	In the NCAA Championship game, Maryland defeats Indiana

Epilogue

Indiana University basketball is not games, opponents or scores. It is not wins or losses. The number of blocked shots or three-point attempts are merely terms describing the sport. IU basketball is much more. It is honor and glory and tradition.

Stories of Hoosier players of different decades share similar themes: boyhood dreams of wearing the red and white, distinct memories of running onto the Assembly Hall court for their first game, the farmer standing on his tractor as crowds of thousands lined Highway 37 to greet returning heroes, life's lessons disguised in basketball settings and hammered into young minds by coaches, the warmth and fraternity of the basketball community regardless of era.

The privileged few who wear the candy-striped pants of the future will experience highs and lows like those who came before them. The scores and opponents will vary. The names and faces will change. The larger legacy of Indiana basketball will endure.

A Player Reflects

"Did we think we had a chance? Yeah. That really goes back to the days of Scott May and Tom Abernethy and Quinn Buckner and Kent Benson and those guys. If those guys don't win that championship the way they did, I don't know that we as a part of Indiana University would have had the same confidence we did. But being a part of the tradition, you step onto that court in any NCAA Tournament, you have that opportunity."

—Chuck Franz
Member of 1981 Championship Team
Guard, 1979 – 1984

Celebrate the Heroes of Indiana and Big Ten Sports
in These Other Acclaimed Titles from Sports Publishing!

Tales from Michigan Stadium
by Jim Brandstatter
- 5.5 x 8.25 hardcover
- 224 pages
- photos throughout
- $19.95
- *2002 release!*

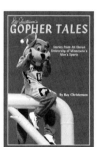

Ray Christensen's Gopher Tales
by Ray Christensen
- 5.5 x 8.25 hardcover
- 200 pages
- photos throughout
- $19.95
- *2002 release!*

Ohio State's Unforgettables
by Bruce Hooley
- 8.5 x 11 hardcover
- 208 pages
- photos throughout
- $29.95
- *2002 release!*

Illini Legends, Lists & Lore: Second Edition
by Mike Pearson
- 10 x 10 hardcover
- 300 pages • 600 photos throughout
- Includes audio CD and a color foldout of the Assembly Hall • $34.95
- *2002 release!*

Jeff Gordon: Burning Up the Track
by the *Indianapolis Star and News*
- 10 x 10 hardcover
- 100 pages
- color photos throughout
- Includes 60-minute audio CD
- $39.95
- *2002 release!*

Tony Stewart: High Octane in the Fast Lane
- 10 x 10 hardcover • 160 pages
- color photos throughout
- Includes 60-minute audio CD
- $39.95
- *2002 release!*

Most Memorable Moments in Purdue Basketball History
by the *Lafayette Journal and Courier*
- 8.5 x 11 hardcover • 247 pages
- color photo section and b/w photos throughout
- $29.95

But They Can't Beat Us: Oscar Robertson and the Crispus Attucks Tigers
by Randy Roberts;
edited by The Indiana Historical Society
- 6 x 9 hardcover
- 200 pages
- 16-page photo section
- $19.95

Glory of Old IU: 100 Years of Indiana Athletics
by Bob Hammel and Kit Klingelhoffer
- 8.5 x 11 hardcover
- 295 pages
- eight-page color photo section
- $34.95

Glory of Old IU: 100 Years of Indiana Athletics (leatherbound edition)
by Bob Hammel and Kit Klingelhoffer
- 8.5 x 11 leatherbound • 295 pages
- eight-page color photo section • $74.95

All copies signed by Isiah Thomas, Scott May, Anthony Thompson, Cynthia Porter, Harry Gonso, Jim Spivey, Jerry Yeagley, Steve Alford, Gary Hall, Mark Lenzi, Bob Hammel, and Kit Klingelhoffer!

To order at any time, please call toll-free **877-424-BOOK (2665)**.
For fast service and quick delivery, order on-line at

www.SportsPublishingLLC.com.